GLOB

The
COSTA
DEL SOL

SUE BRYANT

NEW
HOLLAND

GLOBETROTTER™

First edition published in 2002
by New Holland Publishers (UK) Ltd
London • Cape Town • Sydney • Auckland
10 9 8 7 6 5 4 3 2 1

website: www.newhollandpublishers.com

Garfield House, 86 Edgware Road
London W2 2EA, United Kingdom

80 McKenzie Street
Cape Town 8001, South Africa

14 Aquatic Drive, Frenchs Forest
NSW 2086, Australia

218 Lake Road, Northcote
Auckland, New Zealand

Distributed in the USA by
The Globe Pequot Press, Connecticut

ISBN 1 84330 296 9

Publishing Manager (UK): Simon Pooley
Publishing Manager (SA): John Loubser
Managing Editor: Thea Grobbelaar
DTP Cartographic Manager: Genené Hart
Editor: Thea Grobbelaar
Designer: Lellyn Creamer
Cover design: Lellyn Creamer, Nicole Engeler
Cartographer: Marisa Galloway
Proofreader: Vanessa Rogers
Reproduction by Resolution (Cape Town) and
Hirt & Carter (Pty) Ltd, Cape Town
Printed and bound in Hong Kong by Sing Cheong
Printing Co. Ltd.

Although every effort has been made to ensure
that this guide is up to date and current at time
of going to print, the Publisher accepts no
responsibility or liability for any loss, injury or
inconvenience incurred by readers or travellers
using this guide.

Acknowledgements:
The author would like to thank Carlos de Garriz
and José Antonio Secilla of CyrASA; the Costa
del Sol Tourist Promotion Board; Spanish Tourist
Board; Viva Air; Hotel Alay, Benalmádena; the
Marbella Club; Hotel Alcora, Sevilla; and Autos
Lara, Torremolinos. The publishers would like to
thank María Utrera, of Patronato de Turismo de
la Costa del Sol, for her help.

Front Cover: Traditional boats on Nerja's beach.
Title Page: Ronda's dazzling whiteness is offset
by fields of scarlet poppies in spring.

CONTENTS

MAKE THE MOST OF YOUR GUIDE

Reading these two pages will help you to get the most out of your guide and save you time when using it. Sites discussed in the text are cross-referenced with the cover maps – for example, the reference 'Map B–C3' refers to the Córdoba map (Map B), column C, row 3. Use the Map Plan below to quickly locate the map you need.

MAP PLAN

Outside Back Cover   Outside Front Cover

Inside Front Cover   Inside Back Cover

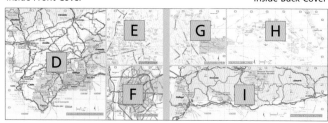

THE BIGGER PICTURE

Key to Map Plan

A – Puerto Banús to Málaga
B – Córdoba
C – Málaga
D – Western Costa del Sol
E – Sevilla
F – Sevilla Area
G – Granada
H – La Alhambra
I – Málaga to Almería
J – Jerez de la Frontera
K – Ronda
L – Gibraltar Town
M – Gibraltar

Key to Symbols

⊠ — address

☎ — telephone

🖋 — fax

🖳 — website

🖱 — e-mail address

🕘 — opening times

🚌 — tour

💰 — entry fee

Map Legend

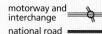

motorway and interchange		main road	Recaredo
national road		other road	Lope de Vega
main road	tarred untarred	railway	
minor road	tarred untarred	built-up area	
river and dam	Río Grande	building of interest	Museo de Belles Artes
route number	N339 431	park & garden	Parque de María Luisa
city	SEVILLA	airport	✈ ✈
major town	⊙ Gibraltar	place of interest	● Finca la Concepción
town	○ Torremolinos	hotel and parador	Ⓗ 🏠 DEL SUR
large village	◎ Tarifa	parking area	🅿
village	○ Lanjarón	post office	⊠
peaks in metres	Castillejos ▲ 1073 m	police station	●
viewpoint	🔆	hospital	⊕
toll road	Ⓣ	place of worship	△ Iglesia de Sta. Cruz
cave	🔴	tourist information	ℹ
ruin	∴		

Keep us Current

Travel information is apt to change, which is why we regularly update our guides. We'd be most grateful to receive feedback from you if you've noted something we should include in our updates. If you have any new information, please share it with us by writing to the Publishing Manager, Globetrotter, at the office nearest to you (addresses on the imprint page of this guide). The most significant contribution to each new edition will be rewarded with a free copy of the updated guide.

Above: *Tourism is the mainstay of the economy on the Costa del Sol.*

OVERVIEW

Spain's 'sunshine coast' forms the southern fringe of the region of **Andalucía**, bordered to the west by the **Tarifa** and to the east by the mountains of **Almería**. With about 320 days of blue sky annually and an endless string of sandy beaches, it's not surprising that over two million tourists a year flock to the area, making it one of Europe's most popular holiday destinations.

Yet despite relentless development, parts of the Costa del Sol still encapsulate all that is Spanish – scented orange groves and rolling fields of silver olive trees; the passion of the bullfight and the rhythm of flamenco; tiny bars where locals sip **Jerez** wines and laughter mingles with the aroma of fried garlic.

The Land
Climate

The Costa del Sol enjoys long, hot summers and mild winters. Humidity is low and summer evenings are balmy. Rain occurs from December to March, but winter temperatures rarely fall below 10–11°C (50–52°F). Away from the coast, the Andalucían summers are less forgiving, and the best time for touring is spring. The Sierra Nevada offers yet another climatic extreme, with heavy snowfall in winter making it Spain's most popular ski area.

Flora and Fauna

The vegetation of the Costa del Sol is typical of the southern Mediterranean, with olives, pine, cork, oak, wheat and sunflowers.

In the Guadalquivir valley, Spain's most expensive and aggressive bulls are bred and trained for the bullring. Here, too, the exquisite Andalucían horses are raised.

History in Brief

Pre-Roman Times

The first known inhabitants lived in caves around what is now Málaga province, leaving wall paintings dating from 25,000BC at **Nerja**, east of Málaga, and at **La Pileta**, near Ronda, of the animals they hunted. Early architecture dating from 2500BC is evident at **Antequera**, where primitive Iberian tribes built cave tombs guarded by massive stones.

Around 1100BC, the **Phoenicians** arrived. **Greek** traders established colonies around 650BC; olives and grapes were introduced at this time. The Greeks were soon ousted by the **Carthaginians**, who moved in and occupied most of Andalucía, using the region's mineral wealth to finance a huge military presence. Under Hannibal, they prepared to attack Rome but were defeated in the Second Punic War in 214BC.

Romans, Vandals and Visigoths

The Romans, welcomed by the Andalucíans in 210BC, began to build on an unprecedented scale. Remnants can be seen in the aqueduct of Nerja, the Roman theatre in Málaga and even the N340 coastal highway, an early version of which connected Cádiz with Rome. The region was named **Baetica** with Córdoba as its capital and 400 years of prosperity followed. Eventually the Roman Empire crumbled and Baetica was invaded by barbarian tribes from northern Europe. First to arrive were the Vandals, who named the area **Vandalusía**, and shortly afterwards the Visigoths, who claimed Roman lands for themselves and ruled for 300 years.

> **Greek Mythology in Andalucía**
> Many Greek myths have origins in Andalucía. **Heracles** (Hercules to the Romans) is said to have opened the Straits of Gibraltar with his bare hands during the tenth of his 12 labours, leaving a pillar on either side. The Guadalquivir Valley was supposed to have been the location of the **garden of the Hesperides**, where the three daughters of **Atlas** lived, and the place from which the **Gorgons**, the **Parcae** and the **Cyclops** originated.

Below: *The burial chambers around Antequera are in a remarkable state of preservation for their age – they are 4500 years old.*

Moorish Influence

The **Moors** saw an opportunity to move into Vandalusía. In AD711, a vast Berber army crossed the Strait of Gibraltar and forced the Visigoths north into the mountains. Some 800 years of Moorish rule followed in the newly named Kingdom of **al-Andalus**.

The tolerant attitude of the Moors meant that Jews, Christians and Muslims lived in harmony and a period of great wealth and cultural development began. Rather than destroying what had gone before, the Moors used Roman buildings as a basis for development, adding their own style to form the astonishingly beautiful monuments that can be seen today in **Córdoba**, **Granada** and **Sevilla**.

In the 11th century, the Christian armies of northern Spain moved in. The Moors needed reinforcements, which unleashed a wave of Islamic fanaticism as the puritanical **Almoravids** from North Africa came into power in 1086. After 60 terrifying years, a more tolerant sect, the **Almohads**, drove them out and set about rebuilding al-Andalus, only to be defeated by the Christians at the Battle of Las Navas de Tolosa in 1212.

The Catholic Kings

In 1492 the last Moorish stronghold fell, **Columbus** discovered the New World, and Spain entered a new era under the dynastic partnership of **Ferdinand of Aragón** and **Isabella of Castile** – *Los Reyes Católicos*, or Catholic kings, as they were dubbed by the Pope. Jews and Muslims were persecuted, and Andalucía deteriorated into a poverty-stricken backwater.

The Twentieth Century

In 1936, **General Francisco Franco** led an army uprising against the government; a civil war followed, causing untold damage to the morale and economy of Spain. In 1939 Franco proclaimed himself head of state and by the end of World War II, Spain was politically isolated from the world.

In the 1950s, American loans were given in return for the right to establish nuclear bases in Spain. This boosted the economy which in turn created a new dawn on the Costa del Sol, an area earmarked for tourism development.

Above: *Franco's rule was a bleak period for many Spaniards.*
Opposite: *Intricate arches are a typical feature of Moorish architecture.*

Government and Economy

Spain is a constitutional monarchy, ruled by **King Juan Carlos**, who is also commander-in-chief of the armed forces. There are 50 provinces in 17 autonomous regions, one of which is Andalucía.

Economic and social problems continue to plague Andalucía which, despite its 'sunshine coast', fosters contrasts between rich landowners and poor workers. The tourism industry has boomed since the first hotels were built in the 1950s, but much of the investment is by foreigners, for foreigners, and there is a strong black economy.

Huge investment has taken place in infrastructure along the coast, including a much needed motorway from Málaga to the west. This will eventually extend all the way to Gibraltar, taking some pressure off the coast road. But housing developments and golf courses continue to spring up at an astonishing pace and environmentalists face a constant battle to maintain any semblance of the 'real' Costa del Sol.

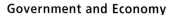

Education in Spain

Education in Spain is free and compulsory for children aged six to 16. There are three stages of school: pre-primary, primary (for ages six to 11), and secondary (for ages 12 to 16). Thereafter, students have a choice between a two-year vocational course or the *bachillerato*, a two year course in preparation for university. There are two types of degree: a *diplomatura* takes three years, and a further two to three years leads to a *licenciatura*. Students who achieve this and write a thesis qualify for a doctorate.

Andalucia has two of Spain's most important universities: Sevilla, which was inaugurated in 1502, and Granada, opened in 1526.

Above: *A farmer taking a break from his labours.*

Convent Cakes
Many of the cakes for which Andalucía is famous are made by nuns, who support their convents by running small cake shops. The tradition stems from the sherry *bodegas* around Jerez, which would use egg whites in the clarification of their wines and give the yolks to the nuns. The influence of the Moors is strong, with honey and almonds creating rich, sweet delicacies.

Málaga has three such establishments: the **Santa Ana** abbey, which specializes in *dulce de membrillo* – quince jelly; **Convento de las Clarisas**, selling quince jelly, coconut balls and lemon turnovers; and the **Asunción** monastery, famous for its *tortas de polverón* (cakes with almonds). On Calle Larios, the main shopping street, the Casa Mira is the city's best-known cake shop.

The People

The Costa del Sol is a cosmopolitan society, with a mix of expatriates, Spaniards and, of course, the occasional exiled crook who contributes to the area's nickname, 'Costa del Crime'. The expatriates, attracted by the climate and relatively high standard of living, actually outnumber Spaniards in some coastal villages such as **Mijas**. The locals are easy-going and tolerant, many of them sustained financially by tourism.

Poverty is a genuine issue and despite improvements in the economy as a result of tourism, Andalucía still has Spain's highest **unemployment** rate at over 25% in some areas. Serious crime is not a threat, but there are reports of an increase in petty crime against tourists at some of the big resorts.

Southern Spain's large **gypsy** population hasn't really integrated into the mainstream. Gypsies follow their own traditions and tend to live in isolated communities. The downside of this is that they are less educated and as a result suffer high unemployment.

Religion

Some 97% of Spaniards are **Catholic**. There is no state religion and small communities of Protestants, Jews and Muslims exist.

Festivals

Every town in Spain has a patron saint, each adding a festival to the calendar. Dates of these festivals vary but the main events take place in Estepona, Benalmádena, Nerja, Torremolinos and Fuengirola between July and October. (*See also* panel on page 87.)

A saint's day is celebrated by a *romería* or pilgrimage to a shrine outside town. Townsfolk parade through the streets, carrying an effigy of the saint. Gradually, the whole town moves out to the shrine for a night of barbecues, vast paellas cooked over a fire, flamenco dancing, singing and dressage competitions. There are firework displays and sometimes a funfair and everybody dresses up in local costume, so it is worth timing a visit to coincide with a local event.

The **Feria de Málaga** is the most spectacular of the festivals, lasting for ten days in August, during which time theatrical events, funfairs, firework displays, bullfights, folk bands and tournaments spring up overnight.

Some festivals are more serious; **Semana Santa**, Holy Week, in Sevilla is slightly eerie, with sombre music and ornate floats depicting scenes from the Passion. Mournful *saetas* are sung and thousands of candles offer the only light. After Easter, Sevilla turns out for **Feria de Abril** (April Fair), a vast celebration of bullfights, flamenco, cultural events and drinking.

The end of April brings **Feria del Caballo** (Jerez Horse Fair), a highlight of the equestrian year. Local breeders, reputed to rear the finest horses in Spain, show off their skills at competitive events and an enthusiastic audience enjoys sherry-tasting. Also in Jerez, **Vendimia** (wine festival) in September follows the blessing of the grape harvest and includes flamenco dancing, bullfights, parades and more equestrian events.

> **Washington Irving**
> Washington Irving (1783–1859), creator of ***Rip Van Winkle***, was the first American author to achieve international fame. His witty, elegant style turned the short story into an art form. Born in New York, Irving studied law, though he always showed more interest in his second career as an essayist for New York papers than for the legal system. Between 1826 and 1829, Irving's legal career took him to Madrid, where he wrote ***Chronicle of the Conquest of Granada***. His most famous work from this period is ***Tales of the Alhambra*** – sketches and short stories written during his stay in the apartments in the palace compound, now a hotel named after him.

Below: *Traditional costumes are worn for the* romería.

Opposite: *La Giralda is an impressive Moorish tower incorporated into Sevilla's grand Gothic cathedral.* **Below:** *In contrast, the city features some striking modern architecture.*

Art and Architecture

For centuries a centre of art and culture, Andalucía's heritage is rich and exciting, with some of the world's most beautiful **Islamic** monuments within reach of the Costa del Sol.

The first remnants of note date back to **Roman** times – the ruins of Italica near Sevilla and the magnificent bronze of a Roman youth in the museum at Antequera. But it was the Moors, arriving in AD711, who made the biggest architectural impact. In Córdoba they built **La Mezquita**, a mosque that was regarded as one of the wonders of the world in its time. Having come from Damascus, centre of the Islamic world, the Moors introduced intricate Arabic calligraphy, brilliant mosaics and structures like **La Giralda** minaret and **Torre del Oro**, a tower tiled in gold in Sevilla. In Granada, the last Moorish kingdom of al-Andalus, **La Alhambra** represents the pinnacle of Moorish culture, palaces of ornate stuccos and exquisitely carved wooden ceilings set among serene gardens and fountains.

The *reconquista* allowed Moorish architecture to continue but with a number of modifications. Gothic and Islamic styles were blended under the Christians to create **Mudéjar**, vividly illustrated in the **Alcázar** (palace) in Sevilla. Later, the 15th-century **Gothic** style was developed into **Plateresque**, featuring the ostentatious use of gold and silver from the New World to adorn every available surface. Granada's **Capilla Real** (Royal Chapel) is Plateresque in style.

Renaissance style arrived in the mid-16th century, a fine example being **Palacio de Carlos V** in the Alhambra at Granada, strangely utilitarian among the intricate Moorish arches and pillars. In the 17th and 18th centuries, architecture swung back to the opulence of **Baroque**. An early example is Granada's cathedral, the façade of which was completed by painter Alonso Cano in 1664.

Fine Art

Most of the work of painters who spent time in southern Spain is in Madrid's **Prado** museum, though some pieces remain in Sevilla and Málaga. Granada's **Capilla Real** has a collection of 15th-century Flemish art belonging to Queen Isabella, including work by **Memling**, **Bouts** and **van der Weyden**, as well as a small **Botticelli**.

Art flourished in Andalucía in the 17th century: **Velázquez** was born in Sevilla, though he left the south aged 24; **Francisco de Zurbarán** arrived in Sevilla in 1628, and **Bartolomé Esteban Murillo** and **José Ribera** worked here. Pieces by all three are in the Museo de Bellas Artes in Sevilla, and in the cathedral, there's a beautiful **Goya** – the story of Santa Rufina and Santa Justa.

With the exception of Goya, who painted scenes from the Plaza de Toros in Ronda, the 18th and 19th centuries were a bleak period culturally for Andalucía. **Picasso** was born in Málaga but left for Barcelona at an early age – Málaga's Museo de Bellas Artes has a selection of his early sketches alongside some **Murillos**, **Riberas** and some fine sculptures.

Goya

Francisco José de Goya y Lucientes (1746–1828), regarded as one of the three greats of his time alongside El Greco and Velázquez, was born near **Zaragossa**. From the age of 14, he studied as an apprentice painter and in 1786 was court painter to Carlos III. Paintings of bullfighting scenes from his days in Ronda with the great bullfighter Pedro Romero are re-enacted every year at Ronda's *goyesca* festival, with matadors in traditional dress. Some of Goya's later works include *The Disasters of War* series from 1810, based on the atrocities of the Napoleonic occupation, and two paintings, *Second and Third of May, 1808*, depicting massacres of unarmed Spaniards by French soldiers. Goya died in **Bordeaux**, France.

Below: *The Costa del Sol stretches out beyond Málaga.*

☆ *See* Map C ★★★

MÁLAGA

By far the best way to explore Málaga's centre is on foot, as the traffic is always busy. Everything shuts down for siesta between 13:00 and 17:00, so early morning or early evening is the best time to explore.

From the bullring at the foot of Gibralfaro hill (*see* page 28), walk along Paseo del Parque past the cream and brown neo-Baroque **Ayuntamiento** built in 1919. Plaza de Aduana, the square of the old Customs House, forms the entrance to the **Alcazaba**, a massive fortress started by the Moors in the 8th century. Just outside the Alcazaba is a **Roman theatre**, excavated in the early 1950s and the only visible Roman structure left in the city.

Within the castle walls is an 11th-century palace, now housing a small **archaeological museum** which includes fragments of pottery from Roman times as well as mosaics and artefacts found locally.

Other sights in Málaga include the **cathedral** (*see* page 34), located a short walk along the Paseo del Parque and up Calle de Molina Lario. A few blocks north-east of the cathedral is the **Casa Natal de Picasso** (*see* page 37). West of the city on the bank of the Guadalmedina river is the **Museo de Artes y Tradiciones Populares** (*see* page 37).

Málaga
🖥 www.andalucia.
com/cities/malaga/
home.htm

Tourist Office
✉ Avda. de Cervantes,
Paseo del Parque.
☎ 95 260 4410
📱 95 221 4120

Town Hall
☎ 95 213 5000

Alcazaba Fortress
🕐 Mon–Sat 10:00–
13:00, 17:00–20:00;
Sun 10:00–14:00
☎ 95 222 7230
💰 Free entrance.

⭐ See Map A–B3   ★ ★ ★

MARBELLA

Marbella has reinvented itself over the decades and is enjoying a new tourism and housing boom as the demand for second homes in the sun rockets. The resort first developed in the 1950s, with the opening of the Marbella Club hotel, and soon became a haunt of the European jet set.

Today, the town is ostentatiously wealthy and glamorous, with its controversial mayor, property developer Jesus Gil, encouraging growth. The old centre, however, continues to be an often overlooked way to spend half a day. The *casco antiguo*, or old town, is very small, its focal point the **Plaza de los Naranjos**, or orange tree square, dating from 1485. Despite umbrellas packing the centre, the geranium-filled balconies and intriguing streets heading off at every angle give the square a feel of another age. Each alley is lined with shops and restaurants to tempt the pocket and the taste buds. The Moorish houses are beautifully preserved, with every street name and house number in colourful ceramic tiles.

On Plaza de los Naranjos is the lovely **Ayuntamiento** (town hall), a graceful 1568 building, with a stone inscription commemorating the reconquest of the town by *Los Reyes Católicos* (*see* page 8) in 1485. Next door is the tourist office, formerly the house of the chief justice, with a façade dating back to 1602. The fountain opposite was placed in the square by the first Christian mayor of the town in 1504.

Main Tourist Office
☎ 95 277 1442
✆ turismomarbella@ctv.es

Plaza de los Naranjos Tourist Office
☎ 95 282 3550

Town Hall
☎ 95 276 1100
✆ 95 282 9015

Marbella Cultural Centre
☎ 95 282 5035

Below: *Plaza de los Naranjos, a good place for a coffee.*

Aloha Golf
⊠ Urbanización Aloha
Golf, 29660 Nueva
Andalucía
☎ 95 290 7085/6
✆ 95 281 2389
✉ aloha@golf-
andalucia.net
🖳 www.
clubdegolfAloha.com

Las Brisas
⊠ Apdo. 147, 29660
Nueva Andalucía
☎ 95 281 0875/3021
✆ 95 281 5518
✉ brisas@golf-
andalucia.net
🖳 www.brisasgolf.com

Los Naranjos
⊠ Apdo. 64, 29660
Nueva Andalucia
☎ 95 281 2428
✆ 95 281 1428/6799
✉ naranjosgolf@
golf-andalucia.net
🖳 www.
losnaranjos.com

Below: *Glamorous
Puerto Banús, a
village-style port
development.*

☼ *See* Map A–A3	★ ★ ★

PUERTO BANÚS

A chic suburb of Marbella, Nueva Andalucía
sprawls across the hills behind the town.
Elegant estates of luxury villas overlook
numerous exclusive golf courses including
Aloha Golf, **Las Brisas** and **Los Naranjos**.
Many of the residents are former inhabitants
of Marbella who have retreated to the hills
in search of privacy.

The main attraction here is **Puerto Banús**.
Whitewashed and candy coloured condominiums, several blocks deep, are grouped
around a large marina filled with luxurious
yachts, while Ferraris and Rolls-Royces cruise
past outdoor restaurants. The people are un-
deniably colourful and sitting at one of the
bars watching the world go by is a popular
pastime. Puerto Banús has not escaped the
advance of mass tourism, however, and souvenir shops and a huge cinema complex are
intermingled with designer boutiques. The
port is currently being extended to accom-
modate transatlantic cruise liners, which will
bring more crowds into the area.

☆ *See* Map M	★★★

GIBRALTAR

A massive chunk of ancient limestone thrust up from the sea bed and flipped on its back some 200 million years ago, Gibraltar forms a tiny peninsula between the town of **La Línea de la Concepción** on the Costa del Sol and the industrial city of **Algeciras**. Just 6km (4 miles) long, 2km (1¼ miles) wide and a towering 450m (1476ft) high, Gibraltar guards the entrance to the Mediterranean. The narrow strait is the only inlet through which Atlantic water can flow into the Mediterranean.

Above: *Gibraltar's dramatic cliffs can be seen for miles.*

Accessible by road or the cable car which leaves from the Alameda Gardens on Main Street, the **Upper Rock Nature Reserve** contains some 600 species of plants, some endemic to Gibraltar. There are several attractions in the reserve. The **Great Siege Tunnels**, dug in 1779, are regarded as a spectacular piece of engineering, allowing the British to position their guns at extraordinary heights. This created an advantage during the Great Siege (1779–83) when the Spanish tried, unsuccessfully, to recapture the Rock. **St Michael's Cave** is another worthwhile attraction, particularly the lower part.

Halfway up the Rock are the famous **Barbary apes**, two colonies of macaques. Legend has it that as long as the apes are here, Gibraltar will belong to the British.

After a tour, relax in **Casemates Square**, the former execution ground, now lined with cafés and pubs and surrounded by massive fortified walls. Main Street, with its tax-free shops, leads off the square.

Gibraltar
🚌 Official guides can be booked through the tourist office for the 90-minute tour of Gibraltar, although independent exploration on foot is possible. Do not try to take a car across the border, as parking is difficult.

Cable Car
🕑 09:30–19:00 daily
☎ 350 77 826

Tourist Board
☎ 350 74 950

Tourist Office
☎ 350 74 982

Above: *Casares has views of mountainside and sea.*

Casares Town Council
☎ 95 289 4150
✆ 95 289 4017

Casares Culture Office
☎ 95 289 5092

Grazalema Information Office
✉ Plaza de Espana 11, 11610 Grazalema
☎ 95 613 2225
🕓 10:30–14:00 and 17:00–18:00 Tue–Sun

Zahara de la Sierra Visitors' Centre
✉ Plaza del Rey 3, 11688 Zahara de la Sierra
☎ 95 612 3004
🕓 09:00–14:00 daily

 See Map D–C4/C5 ★★★

PUEBLOS BLANCOS

Each of the *pueblos blancos*, the white towns on the hills west of Marbella, has a typical Moorish configuration – a tangle of narrow streets below a castle, and whitewashed houses opening inwards to shady patios. These towns are a different world from the busy coast and one of the few remaining tastes of the 'real' Andalucía.

Casares, an immaculate *pueblo* suspended from a hillside beneath its castle, is the most accessible of the White Towns. It allegedly takes its name from Julius Caesar, who used to favour the sulphuric springs on the mountain outside nearby Manilva. The spa is ruined now but the strange-smelling water continues to gush out.

Further inland, **Gaucín** is one of the loveliest White Towns. The views from its Moorish fortress over the coastal plain to Gibraltar and Morocco are breathtaking. While there is little of historical interest in the town, it is pleasant for a stroll and a drink.

Grazalema, a sleepy little village near Ronda, seems suspended from a bare cliff face. It is famous for its hand-woven blankets, and a couple of shops around the busy main square sell the soft woollen products of a small factory outside the town.

The sugar cube houses of **Zahara de la Sierra** spill down a conical hill topped by an 800-year-old Moorish castle. Built by Moors in the 8th century, the village has been designated a national monument.

☆ *See* Map K	★ ★ ★

RONDA

Ronda is one of the oldest towns in Spain and also has one of the most dramatic locations – slashed in half by **El Tajo Gorge**. The town is associated historically with bandits and bullfighters. The bullring here is one of the oldest in Spain and was where the great matador **Pedro Romero** lived, fought and died. Bandits roamed the mountains in the 19th century, robbing wealthy tourists headed for Ronda on their Grand Tour of Europe. In the 20th century, Ronda held a fascination for writers and bullfighting enthusiasts from far afield. **Ernest Hemingway** wrote two books in particular which feature the town: *For Whom the Bell Tolls* and *Death in the Afternoon*. Actor **Orson Welles** is buried here.

Three bridges span the El Tajo Gorge. The original Moorish structure, **Puente de San Miguel**, looks down on the well-preserved 13th-century **Arab baths**. Next to it, the **Puente Viejo** was built in 1616. The **Puente Nuevo**, the new bridge, dates back to 1788 and has dramatic views of the gorge and the plains beyond. The gorge itself, not surprisingly, has a gruesome past. One of its victims was the architect of the Puente Nuevo, who fell to his death while reaching for his hat, blown away by a gust of wind. Apart from countless suicides, Republican sympathizers were thrown into the gorge during the Spanish Civil War by Franco's troops and in the 18th century, injured horses from the bullring were flung over the cliff.

Ronda Information Office
✉ Casa del Guarda, Paseo de la Alameda S/N, 29400 Ronda
☎ 95 287 7778
🕐 08:00–15:00 Mon–Fri

Tourist Office
☎ 95 287 1272 or 657 2636

Arab Baths
🕐 10:00–14.00 and 16:00–19:00 Tue–Sat, 10:00–14:00 Sun

Bullfighting Museum
☎ 95 248 5248

Below: *The three bridges spanning Ronda's gorge are stunning feats of architecture.*

Antequera
🖰 turismo@
aytoantequera.com
🖵 www.aytoantequera.
com

Tourist Office
☎ 95 270 2505

Cueva de Menga
🕓 10:00–14:00 and
15:00–17:30 Tue–Fri,
10:00–14:00 Sat–Sun
💰 Entry is free.

Museo Municipal
🕓 10:00–13:30
Tue–Sat
☎ 95 270 4051

See Map D–E3   ★ ★ ★

ANTEQUERA

This charming 5000-year-old city is a gem, with architecture from the Romans, Moors, Christians and even Neolithic Man. An hour's drive north of Málaga, it can be combined with a visit to **El Torcal** (*see* page 40).

Some of the oldest **dolmens** – prehistoric tombs – in Europe have been found here. Three of these, located around the city's northern outskirts, are open to the public, the most impressive being **Cueva de Menga**. How the huge rocks were cut and dragged into place to form crude caves remains a mystery, similar to that of Stonehenge in the UK.

Antequera is best seen from the Moorish **Alcazaba** which overlooks the city and the plain beyond. The gardens of the ruined Alcazaba are being restored and alleys of tall cypresses planted, framing magnificent views out across the chequered plains.

The 18th-century **Palacio de Nájera** houses the small **Museo Municipal** (*see* page 37). It contains a bronze sculpture of a Roman boy, dating from the 1st century AD and said to be one of the most important pieces of its kind ever to be found in Spain. A peasant stumbled on it in a field one day and his plough cut off the thumb of the right hand, but otherwise the statue is intact.

The museum also houses gold and silverware belonging to the various orders of monks that have inhabited the city. The ground floor gallery contains the work of **Cristóbal Toral**, an Antequeran artist whose paintings are exhibited all over the world.

Below: *Lovers' Rock rises majestically out of the plains beyond Antequera.*

☆ See Map I–C2   ★★★

FRIGILIANA

High in the hills behind Nerja is Frigiliana, a gem of a village which won the 1992 award as the most beautiful village in Andalucía. After the *reconquista*, it became a **Morisco** settlement, inhabited by **Moors** who had been forced to convert to Christianity. Eventually all the Moors, including the Moriscos, were expelled from Spain, and the sad tale of their persecution is told by a number of coloured ceramic murals that are dotted around the ***barrio morisco***, the immaculately preserved old part of the village.

Below: *Frigiliana, a perfectly preserved Moorish village.*

Despite the fact that it is a popular tourist attraction, Frigiliana retains all its charm – donkeys clatter through the narrow streets and gypsies call out to the elderly householders, offering items for sale. Every balcony is a riot of colour and scarlet geraniums tumble out of ceramic pots framing each doorway. There are shops and bars in the lower part of town – the only area navigable by car – selling ceramics, mountain honey, olive oil and wine. For the best view, climb up to the *mirador* (lookout point), offering spectacular views of the orchards and coast. There is a little bar and barbecue at the top.

Frigiliana Tourist Office
⊠ Plaza del Ingenio S/N
☎ 95 253 3126
🖳 www.ayto-frigiliana.com

Town Council
⊠ C/Real 80
☎ 95 253 3002

Taxis
⊠ Plaza del Ingenio
☎ 95 253 3231, 253 3138 or 253 3048

Above: *The narrow streets of Jerez are deserted at midday.*

☼ *See* Map J   ★ ★ ★

JEREZ DE LA FRONTERA

Jerez de la Frontera is famous for two reasons: wine and horses. These go hand in hand – wealthy wine growers who have lived in the area for generations set up vast country estates and were quick to adopt pursuits like breeding thoroughbreds to match their lifestyle. Jerez horse and wine society is notorious among Andalucíans for its airs and graces.

The **sherry *bodegas*** are a highlight of Jerez. Each *bodega* has a tradition of celebrity autographs on its dusty old barrels and visitors to González Byass, for example, will spot the signatures of General Franco and Orson Welles. Tours demonstrate the sherry- and brandy-making process and end with a tasting, based on the saying: 'if you don't have a *copa* by eleven, you must have eleven at one'. The wine is aerated by pouring it with a flourish from a height of one metre into tiny glasses known as *copitas*.

The **Royal Andalucían School of Equestrian Art**, next to a 19th-century palace in a beautiful park, is regarded as one of the top dressage schools in the world. The Spanish thoroughbred is ideally suited to the intricate movements of *haute école*, or High School dressage. The spectacular **Sinfonía Caballo** (*see* panel, this page), which the Spanish describe as a 'horse ballet', is a performance similar to that of the Spanish Riding School in Vienna. Alternatively, you can watch the horses in training and tour the stables and tack room.

Jerez de la Frontera Tourist Office
☎ 95 633 1150

Sherry *Bodegas*
🚌 Tours of the sherry *bodegas* are run on most days, except during August. Advance booking is essential.

Royal Andalucían School of Equestrian Art
☎ 95 631 1111
🕐 Mar–Oct

Sinfonía Caballo
🕐 Performances 11:00 Tue and Thu (book in advance)
🕐 Stables and tack room 11:00–13:00 Mon–Wed and Fri

See Map E–B2   ★ ★ ★

LA GIRALDA, SEVILLA

La Giralda, a **Moorish minaret** dating back to the 8th century, has become the symbol of Sevilla and is all that remains of the mosque built by the Arab conquerors. The name Giralda comes from the *giradillo* (the bronze weather vane) on the top of the minaret, representing 'faith'. A life-sized replica can be found inside Sevilla's cathedral (*see* page 35).

Inside the tower, a series of ramps – wide enough to let the Moors ascend on donkeys – leads to the top, 94m (308ft) above the city with 360-degree views. The Moors used to have an observatory up here, as well as using the minaret for the call to prayer. The top of La Giralda is in fact newer than the base; in the 14th century an earthquake damaged four ornamental globes that used to be here, and in the 16th century a belfry was installed.

At the base of the tower, the **Patio de los Naranjos**, or orange tree patio, is the only other surviving part of the mosque. The patio contains the irrigation channels that would have filled the fountain in which the faithful washed themselves five times a day.

The other Moorish relic of note in Sevilla is the **Torre del Oro** (*see* page 36).

Sevilla Tourist Office
☎ 95 422 1404

Municipal Information Centre
☎ 95 423 4465

La Giralda
🕐 10:30–17:00 Mon–Sat, 14:00–18:00 Sun
🖥 www. andalucia.com/cities/ seville/giralda.htm
🖥 www. sol.com/monumentos/ giralda.htm

Below: *La Giralda's minaret, which was used to call the Moors to prayer.*

See Map E–A2 ★★★

Sevilla Tourist Office
☎ 95 422 1404

**Municipal
Information Centre**
☎ 95 423 4465

The Alcázar
✉ Plaza del Triunfo,
Sevilla
☎ 95 442 7163
🖥 www.sol.com/
monumentos/
index-es.htm
🕐 09:30–17:00
Tue–Sat, 09:30–13:30
Sun and holidays.

THE ALCÁZAR, SEVILLA

This is one of the best surviving examples of **Mudéjar** architecture, a part-Arab, part-Gothic and part-Renaissance style adopted by the Moors who worked under the Christians. Most of the building today is the work of the 15th-century King Pedro the Cruel, although subsequent inhabitants have left their mark. **Isabella I** added a wing in 1503, from where the negotiations for Columbus' voyages were carried out, and **Charles V** added a series of state apartments later in the 16th century. Most of the palace is open to the public.

The building is adorned with exquisite mosaics and paintwork, particularly the red, gold and green half-dome ceiling in the opulent **Salón de los Embajadores**, where Queen Isabella received Columbus. Lions, castles and animal figures, however, give the style away; Moors would never have used such symbolism in their own designs.

In the Chapel, **Alejo Fernandez'** painting *Virgen de los Mariantes* shows the virgin of the navigators watching over Columbus and his first crewmen. Also fascinating is **Patio de las Muñecas** (Patio of the Dolls), so-called because of tiny doll faces carved on some of the arches. It was the **harem** in the original palace and the shuttered windows, *celosias* or *jalousies*, take their name from this era, when women could see out but no-one could see in.

The gardens, filled with flowering plants, are a mass of exotic perfumes in spring.

Below: *Sevilla's Alcázar is a classic example of Mudéjar architecture.*

☆ *See* Map H	★ ★ ★

LA ALHAMBRA, GRANADA

The Alhambra is one of the most important Moorish palaces in the world. There are three main sections to explore: the **Alcazaba** and the palace of Charles V; the **Casa Real**, or Royal Palace; and the **Generalife Gardens** (*see* page 40).

Above: *Patio of the Lions, a tranquil spot in the Alhambra.*

Little remains of the original **Alcazaba** other than walls and foundations, though the watchtower **Torre de la Vela** has magnificent views across the Darro valley to the Albaicín, the old Arab quarter of the city.

The **Royal Palace** is the highlight of the Alhambra. The first section opens out into the **Patio de los Arrayanes**, the Court of Myrtles, with a goldfish pool and fountain flanked by myrtle hedges. Off the patio are two magnificent rooms, the **Sala de la Barca**, with a wooden ceiling shaped like an inverted boat hull, and the **Salón de los Embajadores**, the Hall of the Ambassadors.

One of the most tranquil parts of the inner palace is the **Patio de los Leones** (Patio of Lions). Twelve lion statues around a central fountain represent the 12 tribes of Israel. Each lion is marked with the Star of David. Four channels flowing from the fountain represent four rivers in heaven (honey, milk, water and wine), and the 124 intricate columns around the patio again represent the seventh heaven, as the sum of the numbers one, two and four make seven.

Granada Tourist Information Office
☎ 95 822 6688
📠 95 822 8916

La Alhambra
🕓 Nov–Feb: 08:30–16:00 daily (ticket office 08:00–17:00), 08:00–21:30 Fri–Sat (ticket office 19:30–20:30); Mar–Oct: 08:30–20:00 daily (ticket office 08:00–19:00), 22:00–23:30 Tue–Sat (ticket office 21:30–22:30).
☎ 95 822 7527
🖥 www.alhambra-patronato.es
🚶 Guided tours take two hours, although it is easy to spend longer. Independent visitors will be allocated a time slot during which they must enter the grounds.

Above: *Hundreds of marble columns in the Mezquita were originally from the Roman and Visigothic churches.*

| ☼ *See* Map B–B2 | ★ ★ ★ |

LA MEZQUITA, CÓRDOBA

This is probably the most spectacular **mosque** ever built by the Moors and still beautifully preserved. Only the mosque at Mecca is larger.

The Mezquita was built by **Abd ar-Rahman I** on the site of a former Visigothic church, itself situated on top of a Roman temple. Started in 736, the original mosque was completed in 796.

The entrance is through the **Patio de los Naranjos**, a square lined with orange trees and the remnants of a fountain. Originally, there was no wall between the patio and the marble columns inside, and the trees represented a continuation of the columns, filtering the sunlight to create a shady place in which to pray and contemplate. The columns, some 580 in total, are mostly marble, topped with red and white horseshoe-shaped arches.

The octagonal **Mihrab** chamber, facing Mecca, was added in the 10th century by al-Hakam II. Brilliant mosaics in gold, red and green, a gift from Byzantine Emperor Nicephoras Phocas II, adorn the walls, elaborate arches forming a dome overhead.

The cathedral, seemingly out of place, was added in 1523 by Charles V, who later regretted tampering with the mosque's simple beauty. The cathedral is worth visiting for its mahogany choir stalls, carved by **Pedro Duque Cornejo**. The **Capilla de Villaviciosa** nearby, built in 1377, is a fine example of Mudéjar architecture.

Córdoba Tourist Information Office
☎ 95 747 1235

La Mezquita
✉ Torrijos S/N
☎ 95 747 0512
🕘 10:00–19:30
Mon–Sat, 14:00–19:00
Sun and holidays.
🖳 www.
andalucia.com/cities/
cordoba/mosque.htm

See Map D–C5/D5 ★★

ESTEPONA AND SOTOGRANDE

A pleasant town 26km (16 miles) west of Marbella, with a long seafront promenade overlooking a wide, sandy beach, **Estepona**'s focal point is **Plaza de las Flores** – a pretty square lined with cafés – off the **Calle Santa Ana**. Remnants of old castle walls and white-washed buildings with red-tiled roofs and geranium-filled balconies in the narrow streets of the old town are the only reminder of the Moorish era that ended 500 years ago.

Estepona supports a large fishing fleet and in the *puerto* fishing boats line up alongside luxury yachts. A lively fish auction takes place every morning, although it's over by 07:00. The covered market on **Calle Castillo** is also worth a visit for the wide range of fresh fruit and vegetables and, of course, fish.

Further to the southwest, **Sotogrande** is a wealthy estate and marina complex with condominiums, hotels and restaurants. Many visitors come to play **golf** on the estate's four exclusive golf courses including **Valderrama**, home of the 1997 Ryder cup. Sotogrande is also the heart of the Spanish polo scene, and boasts Spain's only permanent **polo** field. There are regular matches in July, August and September and practice matches throughout June.

Estepona Tourist Office
☎ 95 280 0913

Sotogrande Town Hall
☎ 95 678 0106 (San Roque), 95 661 5109 (Guadiaro)

Valderrama Golf Club
✉ Avda. de Los Cortijos 1, 11310 Sotogrande
☎ 95 679 1200
📠 95 679 6028
🖰 valderrama@golf-andalucia.net
🖳 www.valderrrama.com

Below: *An atalaya, an ancient watch-tower, is silhouetted in the sunrise over Estepona.*

MálagaTourist Office
☎ 95 260 4410
📠 95 221 4120

Gibralfaro Lighthouse
🕐 09:30–20:00 daily

Gibralfaro Castle
☎ 95 222 7230
🖥 www.andalucia.com/cities/malaga/gibralfaro.htm
💰 Free entrance
🕐 09:00–14:00 and 16:00–19:00 (20:00 in summer) daily

English Cemetery
☎ 95 222 3552
🕐 09:30–13:00 and 14:30–17:30 daily

> ✿ *See* Map C–C1   ★★

GIBRALFARO

A walk up the Gibralfaro hill rising above Málaga gives a superb perspective of the centre and its fortified Alcazaba (*see* page 14) below, with views of the port and the Costa del Sol stretching away to the west. A footpath from the **Ayuntamiento** (town hall) winds up to the 14th-century **Moorish castle** with its solid walls and parapets and the **Moorish lighthouse** which gave the hill its name – Jebel al Faro, or hill of the lighthouse. Málaga's small *parador* (state-run hotel) enjoys spectacular panoramic views from just below the castle.

At the foot of the hill is the 19th-century **bullring**, where Sunday *corridas* attract big crowds and big names. A short walk east of the bullring is the **English Cemetery**, founded in 1830 by British Consul-General, William Mark. Here you can explore the tombstone inscriptions; many date back 150 years, and are written in English.

Right: *Gibralfaro castle is surrounded by shady gardens.*

GIBRALFARO & NERJA

☆ *See* Map I–D3 | ★ ★

NERJA

Nerja is a bustling, easy-going place with an informal feel. Its name comes from the **Moorish** word *naricha*, which means 'rich in water', and the town is surrounded by peach and pomegranate groves.

Despite developing into a holiday destination in the 1960s, Nerja has managed to avoid high-rises and most of the accommodation is in its pretty centre or in whitewashed villas on the hills behind. A car, or at least a bicycle, is a good idea here, as some of the best and most deserted beaches are a short distance away.

Above: *Nerja's elegant promenade, the Balcón de Europa, is a popular place for a stroll.*

Nerja's most famous attraction is the **Balcón de Europa**, a short, palm-lined promenade jutting out over a couple of small coves, with sweeping views of the coast in either direction. A couple of 400-year-old cannons point out to sea. The old part of the town clusters around the promenade and spills over the edge of the cliff, some hotels having uninterrupted views of the coast.

Nerja achieved international fame in 1959 when a group of local schoolboys stumbled on some of the most spectacular underground limestone formations in Europe, complete with Neolithic paintings and tools dating back 27,000 years to 25,000BC. The **Cuevas de Nerja** boast some magnificent stalactites and bizarre rock formations, including one joined column which is said to be the world's largest.

Nerja Tourist Office
☎ 95 253 0782
🖥 www.malagaweb.com/english/nerja.asp

Cultural Centre
☎ 95 252 3863

Nerja Caves
☎ 95 252 9520
🕐 10:00–14:00 and 16:00–18:30 daily

Taxi Service
☎ 95 252 0537

Above: *The church of San Pedro in Arcos de la Frontera, perched on the edge of a sheer cliff.*

🌼 *See* Map D–B4 ★★

ARCOS DE LA FRONTERA

Arcos de la Frontera, high above the river Guadalete, is a whitewashed village that spills down a sheer limestone cliff, its warm sandstone monuments glowing in the sun.

All the important monuments are within easy walking distance of one another; the walls of the **Moorish castle** and the towering Gothic-Mudéjar Church of **Santa María de la Asunción**, built on the site of a former mosque, form two sides of the main **Plaza de España**. The church, built between the 16th and 18th centuries, has a Plateresque south façade with a tall, but unfinished bell tower. A *mirador* (viewing point) on the open side of the square looks out over the plains. The town's *parador* (state-run hotel) is located on this square.

Further into the old town is the Gothic church of **San Pedro**, leaning precariously over the steep cliff face. The 15th-century altar is worth a look. For a good vantage point, climb the tower. Other monuments worth the short walk are **Casa Cuna**, once a synagogue, and the **Iglesia de la Coridad**, a 16th-century church on the square of the same name.

There are relatively few places to eat in the old part of town. Most of the restaurants are at the foot of the hill, which is also the best place to park.

Arcos de la Frontera Tourist Office
☎ 95 670 2264
🖳 www.andalucia.
com/province/cadiz/
arcos/home.htm

Town Hall
☎ 95 670 0002

Taxi Rank
☎ 95 670 1355 or
670 0066

☆ *See* Map A–D2	★

MIJAS

Like many Andalucían villages, Mijas, located in the hills behind Marbella, has **Roman**, **Phoenician** and **Moorish** origins. Its present layout dates from Moorish times, with a tiny section of the fortifying wall visible near the parish church, formerly the site of a mosque. The village served as a **granary** for Fuengirola, a defense stronghold against the Christians (till the surrender of Málaga, when the villagers gave in), and in the 17th and 18th centuries as housing for the workers of the now disused agate and marble **quarries** in the hills. The stone from the quarries was used in Málaga's cathedral and the Alcazaba in Sevilla.

The best time to visit is just before sunset, when the coach parties have headed back down the mountain road, the light is golden and the craft and curio shops are still open. Mijas is small enough to explore on foot, though *burro* (donkey) 'taxis' and carriages wait patiently by the car park to ferry visitors through the narrow streets, which are crammed with craft and souvenir shops selling everything from carved wooden bowls to lace shawls, ceramics and the inevitable T-shirts. A couple of art galleries are worth a browse and the town hall displays the work of local artists, as well as farming tools and artefacts from former generations. For details of the bullring and the bullfighting museum, *see* page 38.

Mijas Tourist Office
☎ 95 248 5900

Bullfighting Museum
✉ C/ Algarrobo 6, 29650 Mijas
☎ 95 248 5548
🕐 10:00–17:30 daily in winter, 10:00–22:00 daily in summer
🎫 Children free

Taxis
☎ 95 247 8288

Below: *Foreign residents outnumber Spaniards in the pretty mountain village of Mijas.*

See Map A–E2 ★

Torremolinos
🖥 www.andalucia.com/
torremolinos/home.htm

Tourist Offices
✉ Plaza Blas Infante 1
✉ Plaza de las
Comunidades
Autónomas, Playa Mar
✉ Plaza de Borbollón,
La Carihuela
☎ 95 237 9512, 237
1909 or 237 2956.
📠 95 237 9551
🖱 turismo@
ayto-torremolinos.org

**Torremolinos Town
Hall**
☎ 95 237 9400
🖱 info@ayto-
torremolinos.org

TORREMOLINOS

Brash, colourful and loud, Torremolinos, the first resort west of Málaga airport, is for the young and lively, with two vast beaches dedicated to sunworshipping, and neon-lit streets that throng with life. The resort is the epicentre of gay life on the coast.

Torre de los Molinos (the Tower of the Windmills) is recorded on a map as early as 1748, when the village was surrounded by 19 flour mills, powered by three streams flowing into the Mediterranean at El Bajondillo beach. The 'torre' itself is an even earlier Moorish watchtower and can still be seen at the end of **Calle San Miguel**.

Today, Calle San Miguel is a riot of bars, pubs, amusement arcades and souvenir shops and leads to a flight of steps descending to the beaches of **La Carihuela** and **Bajondillo**, divided by a rocky promontory. La Carihuela, the original fishing village that used to serve Málaga, still bears traces of its humble past, and fishermen can be spotted here in the morning, grilling sardines over open fires on the beach.

Below: *The lights of Torremolinos shine brightly.*

Despite its largely transient population, Torremolinos has some 30,000 permanent inhabitants who turn out each September for a spectacular *romería* in honour of **San Miguel**, the patron saint. Gypsy caravans, Andalucían horses and flamenco dancers parade through the streets to the forest behind the town, for a night of barbecues, *paella* cooking, *fino* drinking and dancing.

⚙ *See* Map D–C6 | ★

Tarifa
🖳 www.tarifainfo.com/
🖳 www.tarifa.net/
index.html

Tourist Office
☎ 95 668 0913

Weather Forecast
☎ 95 668 1001

Cultural Association
☎ 95 668 0993

Left: *Tarifa's high winds attract many windsurfers from all over Europe.*

TARIFA

An easy day trip from the main resorts of the Costa del Sol, Tarifa is the southernmost point of Spain and supposedly the windiest place in Europe, hence its popularity as a **windsurfing** centre. Surf shops line the main street, and the long beaches and Atlantic breakers are a riot of sails for most of the year. A young, lively culture has sprung up in the town, although the beaches are less attractive to sunbathers as the winds are too strong to sit on the sand for long.

Important Roman remains of the city of Baelo Claudia, built in AD171, have been found at the nearby village of **Bolonia** and are considered among the best preserved in Spain. Tarifa itself is built around a 10th-century **Moorish castle** now named after Guzmán el Bueno (the good), commander of the town in 1292 when it was under siege by Moorish attackers. A Christian traitor had taken Guzmán's son prisoner and threatened to kill him if the town did not surrender. Guzmán threw his own dagger to the Moors and the son was killed, but the town did not fall.

Above: *The impressive cathedral of San Salvador, Jerez de la Frontera.*

Churches and Cathedrals

Málaga Cathedral

Built on the site of an old mosque, the cathedral is locally named La Manquita, or 'one-armed lady', as it has only one tower. It is a national monument. The altar is made of Italian marble, with agate columns, and the 17th-century choir stall was carved by Pedro de Mena.
⊠ Calle de Molina Lario, ☎ 95 221 5917, ⊕ 09:00–18:45 Mon–Sat, except public holidays.

Nuestra Señora del Carmen, Antequera

El Carmen church has been designated a national monument. A former convent and an unimposing Baroque structure from the outside, the church contains a magnificent 12m-high (40ft) wooden altar, built in the middle of the 18th century and covered with gilt in parts but crammed with intricate carvings of angels and saints. The inside of the church is adorned in brilliant colours.
⊠ Callejón de la Piscina, Antequera, ☎ 95 284 1244, 📠 95 284 1244.

San Salvador, Jerez de la Frontera

The cathedral of San Salvador, also known as La Colegiata, is the place where the celebration of the wine harvest begins each September. The building is a mixture of Gothic and Renaissance styles and has a separate bell tower.
⊠ Plaza de la Encarnación, Jerez de la Frontera.

Capilla Real, Granada

This is an impressive Gothic structure with a Renaissance altar, built by Ferdinand and Isabella in 1504. Their burial tombs are simple caskets in a tiny crypt, though a lavish monument above was carved in marble by Italian artist Domenico Fancelli. Panels along the side depict Christ and the Apostles. The figures of the king and queen look similar but Isabella's head, said to be heavier than her husband's because she was more intelligent, sinks much further into her stone pillow. A gilded grille guards the high altar, covered with gold-leaf and illustrating scenes from the lives of the monarchs. Items on display in the sacristy include a silver and gilt jewellery box that was handed to Columbus by Isabella, full of gold coins to finance his expeditions.

✉ *Oficios 3, 18001 Granada,* ☎ *95 822*

7848, ⏱ *10:30–15:00 Oct–Mar, 11:00–13:00 Sun and holidays; 10:30–15:00 and 16:00–19:00 Apr–Sep, 11:00–13:00 Sun and holidays.*

Sevilla Cathedral

This is technically the largest cathedral in the world, with 43 richly decorated chapels. Most impressive is the high altar. Created by Pierre Dancart, the altar is the largest in the world, with gold-leaf covering 44 scenes from the New Testament. Some of the top figures are over 2m (6½ft) tall. The supposed remains of Christopher Columbus are near the entrance to the sacristy.

✍ *arzobispado@ diocesisdesevilla.org* ☎ *95 421 4971.*

The Remains of Columbus

Columbus sailed west from Palos, Spain, in 1492, hoping to discover a new route to Asia. Instead, he landed on a small island in the Bahamas and went on, over the next five years, to discover Cuba, Jamaica, Venezuela, Panama and what is now Haiti and the Dominican Republic.

Sevilla is supposed to be the final resting place of Columbus but no-one knows whether the remains, brought from Havana in Cuba when it ceased to be a Spanish colony, are really his.

Below: *Queen Isabella's dearest wish was to be buried in the Capilla Real in Granada.*

Historic Buildings

Plaza de Toros, Ronda

This bullring is one of the oldest and most revered in Spain. Dating back to 1785, it was the stage upon which Pedro Romero, considered the founder of modern bullfighting, evolved the style of fighting bulls on foot rather than horseback. A festival is held each year in September, the *goyesca*, featuring only the country's best matadors, dressed in 18th-century costumes, and the finest bulls. A small museum inside has bullfighting memorabilia and posters advertising the very first *corrida* in the ring.

⊠ *Plaza de España, Mercadillo, Ronda,* ☎ *95 248 5248,* ⊕ *10:00–18:00 in winter, 10:00–20:00 in summer.*

Palacio de Mondragón, Ronda

This palace was built by Abomelic, King of Ronda, in 1314 and housed subsequent Moorish rulers before Ferdinand and Isabella converted it for their own use after the reconquest. Much of the original stucco work and mosaics remain around the spacious patios with their horseshoe arches. The roof terrace looks out over the plains.

⊠ *Plaza de Campillo, La Ciudad, Ronda,* ⊕ *10:00–19:00 Mon–Fri, 10:00–15:00 weekends and holidays.*

Torre del Oro, Sevilla

The Golden Tower, which stands on the bank of the Guadalquivir river, was built by the Almohads in the 13th century as a guard tower. The 12-sided structure was covered with shimmering gold tiles. Later, it served as a prison and today houses a small naval museum.

⊠ *Paseo de Cristóbal Colón S/N, 41001 Sevilla,* ☎ *95 422 2419,* ⊕ *10:00–14:00 Tue–Fri, 11:00–14:00 Sat–Sun.*

Museums and Galleries

Casa Natal de Picasso, Málaga

The house where Picasso was born holds the Picasso Foundation, managed by the Town Council. The foundation is a centre for research into and exhibition of contemporary art, including works by Picasso. This is not a place to see all Picasso's great works, but it does give one a good insight into the artist's early life and influences.

✉ Casas de Campos, Plaza de la Merced, ☎ 95 206 0215, ⏰ 11:00–14:00 and 17:00–20:00 Mon–Sat, mornings only Sun.

Museo de Artes y Tradiciones Populares, Málaga

Housed in a 17th-century coaching inn situated to the west of the city on the bank of the Guadal-medina River, this museum gives visitors an insight into life

before tourism on the Costa del Sol, with a wood-burning oven, an old *bodega*, or wine cellar, fishing and farming imple-ments and a collection of popular ceramics among its exhibits.

✉ Pasillo de Santa Isabel 10, ☎ 95 221 7137, ⏰ 10:00–13.00 and 16:00–19:00 in winter, 10:00–13.30 and 17:00–20:00 in summer, closed Sat evenings and Sun.

Museo Municipal, Antequera

For further details about Antequera's museum, see page 20.

✉ Palacio de Nájera, Plaza del Coso Viejo S/N, ☎ 95 270 4051, ⏰ 10:00–13:30 Tue–Sat.

Above: *Every tile tells a story in Sevilla's Plaza de España.*
Opposite: *Over 200 years old, Ronda's bullring is known as the cradle of modern bullfighting.*

Picasso

Pablo Picasso was born in Málaga in 1881. He painted his first picture at the age of 10 and by 15 had qualified for a place at the Barcelona School of Fine Art. During his career, he produced over 20,000 paintings, sketches and sculp-tures. One of his most important works illus-trating contemporary Spanish history is *Guernica*, in honour of the Basque town bombed by the Germans. It is in Madrid's museum of 20th-century art.

Above: *The bullring and bullfighting museum in Mijas.*

Museo Taurino Municipal, Antequera

A small bullfighting museum is situated upstairs in Antequera's bullring (the only one in Spain with a restaurant inside its walls). The museum displays stuffed bulls' heads and photos of some of the great matadors of yesteryear, as well as ornate, sequined and brocaded costumes.

✉ Plaza de Toros, ☎ 95 270 0726, ⏰ 17:00–20:00 Sat, 10:00–13:00 and 15:00–20:00 Sun and holidays.

Bonsai Museum, Marbella

For the botanical enthusiast, this museum houses a lovingly tended collection of miniature trees, cultivated in the Japanese style to be perfect, dwarf versions of the real thing. A 300-year-old olive tree and some *pinsapo* firs are the museum's prize specimens, nestling among rocks taken from the El Torcal National Park.

✉ Jardines Arroyo de la Represa, Avenida Dóctor Maiz Viñal S/N, Marbella, ☎ 95 286 2926, ⏰ 10:00–13:30, 16:00–19:00 in winter; 10:00–13:30, 17:00–20:00 in summer.

Museo Taurino, Mijas

Mijas has a bullring (unusual in that it is square), built in 1920, in front of the parish church. There's also a colourful bullfighting museum with interesting scenes of the great matadors and taurean memorabilia.

✉ Algarrobo 6, Mijas, ☎ 95 248 5548, ⏰ 10:00–17:30 daily in winter, 10:00–22:00 daily in summer.

Archaeological Museum, Almuñécar

Located above the main square, Plaza Ayuntamiento, the small archaeological museum is housed in the Cueva de los Siete Palacios, a structure believed once to have been a Roman water reservoir. It displays a number of important local finds, including an Egyptian vase dating from the 17th century BC.

⊠ Follow the signs from the Plaza de la Constitución, ⊕ Mon–Sat 10:30–13:30 and 16:00–18:00 (Oct–Apr), 10:30–13:30 and 18:00–20:00 (May–Sep).

Museo de Bellas Artes, Sevilla

The Fine Arts Museum is Spain's second most important art gallery, after Madrid's Prado, and offers a detailed history of Sevillian painting. It became a museum in 1839 – previously it was a convent, the Convento Casa Grande de la Orden Mercedaria. In the square facing the museum, the Plaza del Museo, is a statue of Bartolomé Esteban Murillo, works of whom can be seen in the museum. Other 17th-century Spanish artists represented in the museum's 15 galleries include Francisco de Zurbarán and Valdés Leal.

⊠ Plaza del Museo 9, ☎ 95 422 0790, ⊕ 15:00–20:00 Tue, 09:00–20:00 Wed–Sat, 09:00–14:00 Sun.

Below: *In the Museo de Bellas Artes in Sevilla is* The Immaculate Conception *by Bartolomé Murillo.*

Fuente de Piedra
North of Antequera is an unusual sight: a breeding colony of **greater flamingo**. Every spring these birds form a sea of pink across the **Laguna de Fuente de Piedra**, a shallow lake with highly saline water which forms Europe's only inland breeding ground for the species. In three hours, it is possible to walk round the lake, past reed beds and marshes which sustain a wide variety of birdlife. A track follows the water's edge all the way back to Fuente de Piedra. Spring is the best time to visit.

Below: *Once a kitchen garden, the Generalife today is a manicured oasis.*

Parks and Gardens
Parque Natural El Torcal, Antequera

A short distance outside Antequera is the extraordinary natural phenomenon of El Torcal – one of the best preserved examples of karst, or limestone scenery, in Europe. The whole area has been designated a national park and there are three walking trails, allowing visitors the opportunity to wander between fantasy rock formations that look like a stack of plates one minute and a human figure the next. Green markers indicate a gentle 45-minute stroll, orange an hour, and red up to three hours. It is essential to stick to the path, as it is all too easy to get lost in this strange moonscape

🖥 *www.cma. juntaandalucia.es*
🕐 *The visitors' centre is open 10:00–14:30 Wed–Sun.*

Finca La Concepción, Málaga

This living museum of exotic plants is set among fountains and statues around a 19th-century mansion with a gazebo. Interesting specimens include a number of rare palms and giant araucaria trees.

✉ *Crta. de las Pedrizas,* ☎ *95 225 2148,* 🕐 *10:00–16:30 Tue–Sun, later closing times in summer.*

El Generalife, Granada

A footbridge leads from the Alhambra to the leafy gardens and patios around the palace. Avenues of cypress trees, pools, ornamental fountains and luxuriant flowerbeds radiating colour make this a perfect place to reflect on the beauty of the Alhambra and admire the views of the city and Albaicín.

✉ *La Alhambra, Granada,* ☎ *95 822 1503 or 822 0912.*

ACTIVITIES
Sport and Recreation

Many visitors use their holiday to learn a new sport, or improve an existing one. **Golf lessons** are available at most courses, and there are specialist golf schools – the Escuela de Golf La Quinta at Marbella, directed by three-time world champion Manuel Piñero, and Atalaya Golf School in Estepona. Benalmádena has a **scuba diving** school operating out of Puerto Marina, taking beginners to a level of proficiency sufficient for open-water dives. Just inland, on Medrana lake, is one of only 70 **cable-ski** centres in the world. This is an ideal way to learn to waterski, with no wake and no waves. Skiers are towed by a rope attached to a wire crossing the lake.

In a country setting on the road to Mijas, the Campo de Tennis run by former Wimbledon champion Lew Hoad (*see also panel, page 76*) has year-round **tennis** courses and tournaments (🖳 www.tennis-spain.com). Spanish star Manolo Santana runs an exclusive tennis club at the Puente Romano hotel.

Riding lessons take place at Los Monteros Hotel Riding School in Marbella (☎ 95 211 3253) and the Lakeview Equestrian Centre at San Pedro de Alcántara (☎ 95 278 6934).

Leaflets on **hiking trails** are available from the tourist board, covering the Sierra Nevada and the Serranía de Ronda. Cross country and downhill skiing, Mountain biking, parapenting and paragliding are also becoming more popular in the area around the Sierra Nevada (*see page 82*).

Polo

Polo originated in **Persia**, where it was played in a rather macabre fashion with the corpse of a goat. The game spread throughout **Turkey** and **Tibet** to **India**, where British army officers learnt to play, this time with a ball. They soon spread the word to the west and polo developed as a rather upmarket pastime, requiring extensive funds to support the necessary string of highly trained ponies.

The warm climate and extensive stabling of **Sotogrande** have been a magnet to polo players since the mid-1980s; British and Argentinian teams train here during their respective winters. Now, for an unusual kind of holiday, complete beginners can try their hand and be practising chukkas within a week.

Below: *There are many opportunities for a game of tennis.*

Above: *Wind- and weather-blasted rocks form bizarre shapes at El Torcal.*

Unusual Costa del Sol

Certain phenomena in Andalucía were once believed to have magical powers. The wind-eroded rocks of **El Torcal**, the gorge of **El Chorro**, and the prehistoric **dolmens** in the region around Antequera were thought to be the work of giants who once inhabited the area, and the drawings of strange animals on the wall of **La Pileta** caves near Ronda were also considered sacred.

Animals were symbolic too – a **bull** signified creative power, while a **horse** meant life after death and a **boar** meant the devil, the destroyer of fields and vineyards. Even plants were symbolic – **olives** symbolized peace, fertility and purification.

Another unusual phenomenon are the 10,000 **cave houses** dotted around Andalucía, 95% of them in the Granada and Almería provinces. Living in a cave became quite popular in the last century, as so many had been hollowed out for mining purposes. The most impressive cave houses are around the town of Guadix, northeast of Granada.

Cave houses are usually built around a single square room with a whitewashed façade, almost like that of a normal house. A chimney and porch are often added to such dwellings, and skylights provide both light and ventilation.

Fun for Children

The Spanish love children and restaurants are happy to serve families late into the evening, a common occurrence here. Many hotels have organized activities for children that allow the adults to have a little freedom on holiday.

There is a growing number of attractions along the coast especially for children. As well as several swimming pools, **Torremolinos Aquapark** (☎ 95 238 8888) has a 'black hole', made up of tubes with sharp drops and turns, the 'kamikaze', arguably the highest water toboggan in Europe, and also a wave pool, a Jacuzzi and a tropical lagoon. Or try the aquapark at **Fuengirola** (*see* panel, this page), which is suitable for children of all ages.

Tivoli World at Benalmádena (☎ 95 244 5044) is a permanent funfair, open year-round, with 36 rides and attractions for even the youngest children. Older children will enjoy the **birds of prey centre** near Marbella (☎ 95 256 8484) or the **aquarium** at Benalmádena Puerto (☎ 95 256 0150).

Travel agents can also book excellent **donkey safaris** around the mountain village of Coín (☎ 95 245 2666); the donkeys trek to an old farmhouse where there are games with prizes for the children.

Leaving from Ronda, which is within reach of most places in the Costa del Sol, there are organized **balloon excursions** around the Serranía and the Sierra de las Nieves.

Parque Acuático Mijas

Children will love the Parque Acuático Mijas in Fuengirola, just outside the town on the Mijas road. Water slides and tubes keep the older children amused, while a separate mini-park caters especially for toddlers. The park is open daily, ⏱ 10:30–17:30 (May), 10:00–18:00 (June and September), 10:00–19:00 (July–August). ⓜ Children under four get in free. ☎ 95 246 0404 or 246 0409

Below: *The Parque Acuático Mijas at Fuengirola is a great day out for children.*

Sevilla's April Fair
Originally intended as a cattle fair, Sevilla's *Feria de Abril* has grown into six days of dancing, *corridas*, horse shows and wine tasting enjoyed by the whole city after Holy Week. Held in specially designated fairgrounds called *Los Remedios*, the fair starts with bullfights and horse parades. Temporary *casetas* – versions of Sevillian country residences – are set up in the fairgrounds, serving wine, tapas and *fino* and playing *sevillanas* day and night. The *feria* is a riot of colour and noise, and people come from all over the region, so book a room well in advance.

Below: *The April Fair in Sevilla is a spectacular festival.*

Walking Tours
Walking Sevilla

One of the best ways to appreciate Sevilla is on foot. All the main attractions are very close together and there is, in fact, not much walking on this tour. (In the intense summer heat, this is probably a blessing.)

Start at the **Torre del Oro** on the banks of the Guadalquivir River. This twelve-sided structure was built by the Almohads as a guard tower in the 13th century and was covered with shimmering gold tiles. Today it serves as a small naval museum.

Walk towards the Puente de San Telmo bridge and turn left into Calle Lobo. Take the third exit from the roundabout at the end, Calle San Fernando, and walk past the lavish Alfonso XIII Hotel, itself a city landmark, to the **tobacco factory** which inspired the opera **Carmen** (*see* panel, page 45). Today it is part of the university.

Cross the road into the park, or **Jardines de los Reales Alcazares**, and cut back to the **Alcázar** (*see* page 24), one of the world's best surviving examples of Mudéjar architecture. Much of what stands on the site today is from the 15th and the 16th centuries. Visitors can see the palace itself, as well as the chapel and the Patio of the Dolls, or **Patio de las Muñecas**. This was the original harem of the palace.

La Giralda (*see* page 23) and the Cathedral (*see* page 35) are adjacent to the Alcázar, and on the opposite side from the gardens. Climb up the series of ramps inside the **Giralda Tower** to the bell chamber, for a stunning view of the city. The construction of the enormous **Cathedral** was started in 1402, and it took 104 years to complete. Within it are a magnificent main altar and also paintings by Murillo, Zurbarán and Goya.

Above: *Trees bearing bitter oranges grow all over Sevilla and Córdoba.*

Next door to the Cathedral on Avenida de la Constitucion is Sevilla's former stock exchange, now housing the **Archives of the Indies**. This is a massive storehouse of maps and documents from many of Spain's great explorers, including Balboa, Pizarro and Cortés. Columbus's logbook and his first correspondence with Ferdinand and Isabella are here.

From here, head deep into the **Barrio Santa Cruz**, where the narrow streets are lined with tapas bars, and open doors reveal tantalizing glimpses of shady green patio gardens. Cross the **Plaza del Triunfo**, heading away from the cathedral, and the **Plaza Virgen de los Reyes**. Turn right into Calle Mateos Gago, where there are several beautiful houses and small bars. Take a right along Calle Meson del Moro, where No. 4 is a restaurant inside an old **Moorish bathhouse**. Cross over Calle Ximenez Enciso and walk down Calle Santa Teresa to the lovely **Plaza Santa Cruz**, one of the prettiest squares in the city.

Opera in Sevilla

Sevilla's romantic image inspired writers and composers throughout Europe and these operas were set in the city:
- *Carmen* (Bizet)
- *The Barber of Seville* (Rossini)
- *The Marriage of Figaro* (Mozart)
- *Don Juan* (Mozart and various other composers; there are no less than 11 versions)
- *Fidelio* (Beethoven and other composers)
- *La Fuerza del Destino* (Verdi)
- *La Favorita* (Prokofiev)
- *Conchita* (Zandonai)
- *Bodas en el Monasterio* (Prokofiev)

Hiking Las Alpujarras

Las Alpujarras is one of the most scenic and beautiful hiking areas in the hinterland of the Costa del Sol. **Lanjarón** and **Capileira** both make good starting points for hikes.

Terraced farming is still practiced here on the vertiginous slopes, and the footpaths are rough and ready, many of them remnants of the old **Camino Real**, the mule tracks which once crisscrossed Spain. Sometimes the paths can be quite hard to see, as they're worn out or covered by undergrowth. Walking in this region, however, will take you through beautiful meadows, alongside gushing streams and through oak and chestnut woods. You will need a good map, tough shoes, a compass and water supplies for independent exploration. Many people, however, prefer to hike with a guide.

Lanjarón is the gateway to the high Alpujarras and is best known as a **spa town**. An easy, six-hour walk is to go from here along the Lanjarón River, which runs perpendicular to the main road, just to the east of town. Walk out of town to the bridge and follow the steep trail upwards. The path meanders peacefully through small farms and meadows, and after about two and a half hours, you will reach a bridge you can cross to return to the town by way of the opposite bank.

Useful Words

Alcazaba • Moorish castle or fortress
Alcázar • Moorish fortified palace
Alameda • promenade or park
Ayuntamiento • town hall
Barrio • quarter or suburb
Carretera • main road
Corrida • bullfight
Cueva • cave
Judería • Jewish quarter
Mirador • lookout point
Mudéjar • style of architecture produced by Moors under the Christians
Plaza de Toros • bullring
Puerto • port
Puerto deportivo • marina
Reconquista • Period between the 8th and 15th centuries when the Roman Catholics reconquered Moorish Spain, mainly in Andalucía.

From **Capileira**, you can hike the amazing **Poqueira Gorge**. This deep gash in the mountainside, its terraced slopes green with crops, is overlooked from high above by the attractive villages of **Bubión**, **Pampaneira** and **Capileira**. Three paths below the village of Capileira cross the river; take the northernmost one, which winds through a villa complex and then traces the river valley for a couple of hours. You can cross the river and return on the other side, or simply turn around and go back.

The lower path outside Capileira leads to **Pampaneira**, a hike of around three hours, after which you can follow a road to **Carataunas** and a further trail to **Orgiva** (this takes another two hours). Orgiva is a lively market town, with a colourful permanent *mercado* (market) every day and also a huge outdoor market on Thursdays. The village is a curious mix of traditional Spanish farmers and new-age travellers, who seem to co-exist peacefully. Buses run from Orgiva back to Capileira.

Alpujarran Rugs
A small cooperative in **Ugíjar**, a town in the Alpujarras, is almost solely responsible for keeping the weaving traditions of the mountains alive. Woollen rugs, bags, ponchos and blankets are made on wooden looms, using images dating back to Moorish times. Birds, fish, animals, plants and geometric shapes are all popular patterns. Further east, in the town of **Macael**, knotted rugs are produced.

Opposite: *Life moves at a slower pace in the high Alpujarras.*
Below left: *Red chilli peppers hanging out to dry in the mountain air.*
Below right: *Visitors can learn yoga and t'ai chi in Bubión.*

Below: *Each Barbary ape on Gibraltar has a name.*

Organized Tours

Local travel agencies and coach companies operate tours all over the coast and the interior, most with a pick up point in **Málaga** city. Coastal destinations include **Nerja**, **Mijas**, **Marbella** and **Gibraltar**, while longer day trips operate to **Granada**, **Sevilla**, **Córdoba**, **Ronda** and **Tangier**. Trips are operated in air-conditioned buses with an English-speaking guide. All the travel agents with offices along the Costa del Sol will book trips to Sevilla and Córdoba – each a day trip and a long coach ride. It's worth staying overnight in both towns to enjoy the atmosphere.

Guidetur, an association of independent, knowledgable guides in Sevilla, will conduct private sightseeing tours. Contact them at ☎ 95 422 2374, ℡ 95 456 1245.

Nevadensis, ☎ 95 876 3127, runs guided walks, pony-trekking and mountain activities.

Sava Travel, ✉ Avenida Bonanza S/N, Benalmádena, ☎ 95 244 4712, offers guided tours to Ronda, Granada, Gibraltar and Sevilla, and they will pick up visitors from each resort.

Yasmine Line Travel, ✉ Avenida Alay Local 27, Benalmádena Costa, ☎ 95 244 5576, ℡ 95 256 1627, has regular excursions to Tangier and Gibraltar.

In Marbella, you can contact **Mountain Bike Aventura**, ✉ Pueblo Platero 8, Bloque 1, Elviria Las Chapas, Marbella, ☎ 95 283 1204, for mountain bike hire and guided tours in rural areas close to the coast.

Autos Lara Jeep Safari, ⊠ Calle Salvador Allende S/N, Torremolinos, ☎ 95 138 1800, 📠 95 238 1081, offers full-day jeep tours daily to El Chorro Gorge and to Parque Ardales.

Tours of Gibraltar are operated by the **Bland Group**, ⊠ Cloister Building, Irish Town, Gibraltar, ☎ 350 77 012. For a taxi tour of Gibraltar, ☎ 350 42 400.

Book your **sherry bodega** visits in Jerez in advance, either direct or through your hotel. **Domecq**, ☎ 95 633 1800; **Fernando de Terry**, ☎ 95 685 7700; **Gonzáles Byass**, ☎ 95 634 0000; **Harvey's**, ☎ 95 615 1030; **Luis Caballero**, ☎ 95 686 1300; **Osborne & Duff Gordon**, ☎ 95 685 5211; **Williams & Humbert**, ☎ 95 634 6539.

In Jerez de la Frontera, tours of the **Royal Andalucían School of Equestrian Art** are popular and need to be booked well in advance; ☎ 95 631 1100. Performances take place on Tuesdays and Thursdays (excluding holidays) at 12:00 and rehearsals on other weekdays.

For guided tours to Ronda, try **Pullmantur**, ☎ 95 238 4400 (in Torremolinos).

In the Nature Park of Grazalema, **Turismo Rural de Bocaleones** operates mountain biking, hiking, trekking and horseriding tours; ☎ 95 612 3114.

Above: *Ronda perches on the lip of El Tajo gorge.*

Ballooning

Marbella-based company **Aviación del Sol**, ☎ 95 287 7249, arranges hot-air balloon trips over the coast and mountains. An evening flight over Marbella and the surrounding resorts is followed by champagne and tapas on landing. The views across the Strait of Gibraltar at sunset are breathtaking, while a pre-dawn trip over the stunning Ronda mountains and the White Towns is finished in style with a champagne breakfast.

Right: *Ceramics are a good buy; look for 'ceramica' signs on the main roads.*

Buying Leather

Nestled at the end of a blind valley, the town of **Ubrique** might seem a surprising place to find *haute couture* leatherware but if you need a new set of luggage or a quality leather wallet, a detour is worthwhile. Ubrique has been exporting cured skins since Roman times, when its products were famous across the Roman Empire. The Moors refined the art, using decorated leather from Morocco on furniture, cushions and ceilings.

Today, many shops sell leather luggage, clothing and accessories bearing the label '**Piel de Ubrique**' or 'real Ubrique', which means that the item is at least 80% handmade.

Shops

Marbella's main shopping street is Avenida Ramon y Cajal, lined with boutiques and designer stores. Craft stores are around the Plaza de los Naranjos. **Puerto Banús** has designer shops and souvenir stalls. **Mijas** and **Benalmádena Pueblo** also have arts and crafts shops.

Agora Bookshop

A variety of books.
⊠ c/Carretería 92, Málaga, ☎ 95 222 8699.

Aliana Bookshop

Sells mainly textbooks and educational books.
⊠ c/Brahms 6, Málaga, ☎ 95 223 5228.

Choi Bisuteria-Marroquineria

The place for fashion items such as leather bags and jewellery.
⊠ c/Miguel Cano, local 5, Marbella, ☎ 95 286 7147.

Confitería Fuente Olletas

Sells delicious home-made sweets and cakes. *Tarta malagueña* is a particular speciality.
⊠ c/Alameda de Barcelo 42, Málaga, ☎ 95 265 3381.

Cristina Lozano

Sells children's wear and accessories.
⊠ c/Enrique Cantos 3, Marbella, ☎ 95 282 0040.

Disco 2000

Offers many musical styles, from classical and flamenco to jazz and film soundtracks. This shop is also an outlet for concert tickets.

⊠ Avenida Ramon y Cajal 2, Málaga,
☎ 95 277 0708,
✆ 95 288 4495.

Farmafer Linense

Sells a variety of health foods.

⊠ Centro Comercial La Cañada 9, Marbella,
☎ 95 286 0828.

Mariella Ladies Boutique

Sells ladies' leisurewear, swimwear and accessories.

⊠ Edif. Farmacia, Urb. Calypso E-29649 Mijas Costa, Málaga,
✆ 95 293 4823.

Prestige Antiques

This shops sells antique furniture and decorative objects, and also offers a free valuation service.

⊠ Calle Cuesta 9, E-29640, Fuengirola, Málaga,
☎ 95 259 3740.

Suyay Gift Shop

This shop sells gifts from South America: leather sculptures, hand-painted ceramics, textiles and small pieces of furniture.

⊠ c/Jacinto Benavente, Málaga.

The Horse Shop

This shop sells quality equestrian products.

⊠ Escuela de Arte Ecuestre, Estepona,
☎ 95 280 8077,
✆ 95 280 8078,
⌂ arteecue@ctv.es

Trajes Flamencos El Camino

Wildly colourful Flamenco dresses as well as other traditional costumes are on sale here.

⊠ c/Estacion 3, in the commercial centre of Hotel Cristobal, Marbella, ☎ 95 282 2002.

Women's Secret

Women's lingerie, reasonably priced underwear and pyjamas.

⊠ Centro Comercial Larios, Avenida de la Aurora 25, Málaga,
☎ 95 236 9393.

Opposite: *Chorizo sausages and pungent cheeses are good buys in markets along the coast.*

Markets
Benahavís

This market sells local arts and crafts, as well as jewellery and gifts.
⊠ *Opposite Los Abanicos restaurant,* ☎ *95 285 5039,* ⏰ *19:00–00:00 Thu–Sat, 16:00–00:00 Sun.*

Estepona

A well-organized market takes place in the town centre every Wednesday, with a great variety of stalls. Get there early. (There's another market around the small port on Sundays.)
⊠ *Avda. Juan Carlos I,* ☎ *95 280 0946,* ⏰ *09:00–14:00 Wed.*

Fuengirola

On Saturday mornings and Tuesdays there is a huge flea market that sells everything from cheap clothing to antique watches. Watch out for pickpockets. (There is another market on Sundays in Fuengirola's port area.)
⊠ *Recinto Ferial (fair site).*

La Línea de la Concepción

Every Wednesday there is a huge, well-organized market in La Línea near the Gibraltar border. Countless bargains can be found, and there is free parking as well as a few eateries nearby.

Málaga

The Málaga *rastro*, or flea market, takes place on Sundays. (The city also hosts local markets every day of the week in each district.)
⊠ *Near La Rosaleda football stadium.*

Marbella

There's a good flea market at the bullring of Nueva Andalucía on Saturdays. (On Monday mornings there is another market near the football stadium.)
⊠ *Nueva Andalucía bullring.*

Nerja

A weekly market is held on Tuesdays in Calle Chaparil, and

there is also a car-boot sale on Sundays. Every evening during the summer months a craft market is held on the Balcón de Europa.

San Luis de Sabinillas

There is a large, rather disorganized market in San Luis de Sabinillas on Sundays, offering countless bargains. Parking is scarce, so go early. (There is also a small market in the town on Fridays.)

⊠ Next to the N340.

Sotogrande

On Sundays there is a small but interesting art and craft market that takes place in the port area of Sotogrande; it is not usually very crowded, which makes it a pleasant shopping experience.

🕐 10:00–15:00 Sun.

Torremolinos

Every Thursday there is a market (El Calvarío) in Torremolinos.

⊠ Near the Town Hall (Ayuntamiento), Torremolinos.

Almería Pottery

Pottery has always been vital in the arid Almería province because of the need to store water effectively. Several towns produce a unique style of earthenware using techniques unchanged for centuries. In **Vera**, the clay is almost white and the shapes inspired by Arab, Phoenician and Byzantine forms. **Albox** produces elegant water pitchers and **Sorbas** produces rustic ceramics and tiles. **Níjar** and **Tabernas** also specialize in un-glazed pottery, usually for holding water. All of these styles can be found in Almería's shops and markets.

Above: *Accommodation is plentiful on the Costa del Sol.*

Paradores

These are government-run hotels in historic or scenic locations, offering the opportunity to stay in a castle or palace at reasonable rates.

The first *parador* was developed in 1926 under the supervision of King Alfonso XIII and today there are 85, including seven on or near the Costa del Sol. They are divided into categories: **natural**, **coastal** or **monumental** settings. *Paradores* along the Costa del Sol include: Parador de Málaga Gibralfaro; Parador de Granada, located inside the Alhambra; Arcos de la Frontera, in a dramatic clifftop location and Ronda, overlooking the gorge. Modern *paradores* are located at Torremolinos, Nerja and Antequera.

WHERE TO STAY

Hotels in the Costa del Sol are rated with a star system, with five stars being the highest rating. '*Gran Luxe*' signifies a particularly luxurious hotel. **Apartment hotels** follow the same grades, the only difference being that they have cooking facilities in the rooms. *Hostals* and *pensiones*, which are more basic establishments, are graded from one to three stars. **Camp sites** are rated either luxury, first, second or third class and are plentiful. Each region, however, is responsible for its own classification, so accommodation gradings will vary. Most villages have rooms for hire – look out for signs saying '*se alquilar*'. Anybody wanting to stay in a protected area, either camping or in a mountain refuge, should contact the **environmental protection agency: RAAR**, ✉ Apdo 2035, 04080 Almería, ☎ 95 126 5018, ℻ 95 126 4240.

Paradores (*see* panel, left) are usually in historical buildings or areas of outstanding natural beauty. Contact **Paradores de Turismo**, ✉ c/Requena 3, 28013 Madrid, ☎ 91 516 6666, ℻ 91 516 6657.

Estancias de España, a private association of hotels and restaurants in historic buildings, produces a brochure detailing its 44 members, 15 of which are in Andalucía. **Estancias de España**, ✉ c/Menendez Pidal, 31, bajo izqd, – local 28036 Madrid, ☎ 91 345 4141, ℻ 91 345 5174.

Antequera

Parador de Antequera (Map I–A1)
Whitewashed *parador* with pool, quiet area.
⊠ *Garcia del Olmo S/N, Antequera,* ☎ 95 284 0901, ✆ 95 284 1312.

Carratraca

Hostal El Principe (Map D–E4)
Characterful *hostal* in a palace. Bargain rates as only one room has private facilities.
⊠ *Antonio Rioboo 11, Carratraca, Málaga,* ☎ 95 245 8020, ✆ 95 245 8101.

Córdoba

• *LUXURY*
Parador de Córdoba (Map D–D1)
Modern *parador*, set in quiet grounds.
⊠ *Avda. de Arruzafa, Córdoba,* ☎ 95 727 5900, ✆ 95 720 0409.

• *MID-RANGE*
Hotel Marisa (Map B–B2)
Simple hotel, opposite La Mezquita.
⊠ *c/Cardenal Herrero 6, 14003 Córdoba,* ☎ 95 747 3142.

• *BUDGET*
Hostal Maestre (Map B–B2)
Charming hostel off the Plaza del Potro.
⊠ *c/Romero Barros 4, 14003 Córdoba,* ☎ 95 747 2410.

Estepona and Surrounds

• *LUXURY*
Golf Hotel Guadalmina (Map A–A3)
Near Marbella; ideally located for Nueva Andalucía golf courses.
⊠ *Hacienda Guadalmina, 29678 S. Pedro de Alcántara,* ☎ 95 288 2211, ✆ 95 288 2291.

Hotel Atalaya Park (Map A–A3)
Well located four-star; fine sporting facilities.
⊠ *Ctra. Nac 340 km168, Estepona,* ☎ 95 288 4801, ✆ 95 288 5735.

Kempinski Resort Hotel Estepona (Map D–D5)
Good hotel with a lavish spa and a beach.
⊠ *Ctra. de Cádiz km159, Estepona,* ☎ 95 211 3306, ✆ 95 211 3465.

• *MID-RANGE*
Hotel El Pueblo Andaluz (Map A–A3)
Hotel built around an old Andalucían house, near the beach.
⊠ *Ctra. Nac 340 km172, 29600 S. Pedro de Alcántara,* ☎ 95 270 0597, ✆ 95 278 9104.

• *BUDGET*
Hostal El Pilar (Map D–D5)
Small, cozy hostel.
⊠ *Plaza Las Flores, 29680 Estepona,* ☎ 95 280 0018.

Gibraltar

• *LUXURY*
Caleta (Map M–C2)
Italian restaurant, wonderful sea views.
⊠ *Catalan Bay,* ☎ 350 76 501, ✆ 350 42 143.

Eliott (Map L–B2)
Deluxe hotel in tree-lined area, near shops.
⊠ *Governor's Parade, Gibraltar,* ☎ 350 70 500, ✆ 350 70 243.

The Rock (Map M–B3)
Set in tropical gardens, with spectacular views.
⊠ *Europa Rd,* ☎ 350 73 000, ✆ 350 73 513.

- *MID-RANGE*

Bristol (Map L–B2)
Pool, lovely garden.
✉ 10 Cathedral Sq,
Gibraltar, ☎ 350 76
800, ☏ 350 77 613.

Granada
- *LUXURY*

**Hotel Alhambra
Palace** (Map H–C3)
Romantic views and
Moorish design.
✉ Peña Partida 2,
18009, ☎ 95 822 1468,
☏ 95 822 6404.

Hotel la Bobadilla
(Map I–B1)
Country estate, 30
minutes from Granada.
✉ Finca la Bobadilla,
Loja, ☎ 95 832 1861,
☏ 95 832 1810.

**Parador Nacional
San Francisco**
(Map H–E2)
In old, gracious convent
inside the Alhambra.
✉ Real de la
Alhambra, ☎ 95 822
1440, ☏ 95 822 2264.

- *MID-RANGE*

**Hotel Washington
Irving** (Map H–E3)
Charming hotel in the
Alhambra, where the
celebrated author
used to live and write
(see panel, page 11).
✉ Paseo de Generalife
2, Granada, ☎ 95 822
7550, ☏ 95 822 8840.

- *BUDGET*

Hotel América
(Map H–D2)
Small hotel in the
Alhambra, cheaper
than the parador.
✉ Real de la Alhambra
53, Granada, ☎ 95 822
7471, ☏ 95 822 7470.

Jerez de la Frontera
- *LUXURY*

Hotel Jerez
(Map D–A4)
Luxurious four-star.
✉ Avda. Alvaro
Domecq 35, ☎ 95 630
0600, ☏ 95 630 5001.

Royal Sherry Park
(Map D–A4)
Modern four-star
located in quiet area.
✉ Avda. Alvaro
Domecq 11, ☎ 95 630
3011, ☏ 95 631 1300.

- *MID-RANGE*

Capele (Map J–C3)
Near sherry bodegas.
Lively bar, restaurant.
✉ c/Corredera 58,
☎ 95 634 6400.

- *BUDGET*

Hostal San Andres
(Map J–C2)
Near sherry bodegas.
✉ c/Morenos 12,
☎ 95 634 0983,
☏ 95 634 3196.

Las Alpujarras
- *MID-RANGE*

**Villa Turistica del
Poqueira** (Map I–F2)
Comfortable hotel run
by local cooperative.
✉ 18412 Bubión,
Granada, ☎ 95 876
3111, ☏ 95 876 3136.

- *BUDGET*

Mesón Poqiera
(Map I–F2)
A basic hostel, with an
excellent restaurant.
✉ c/Doctor Castilla 6,
18413 Capiliera, Gran-
ada, ☎ 95 876 3048.

Málaga
- *LUXURY*

Málaga Palacio
(Map C–B2)
Four-star with pool;
near shops and sights.
✉ Cortina de Muelle 1,
☎ 95 221 5181.

Parador de Málaga-del Golf (Map A–E1)
Modern *parador* on the beach, near airport. Spacious grounds with very good 18-hole golf course and golf school. ✉ Apartado de Correos 324-29080 Málaga, ☎ 95 238 1255, ℡ 95 238 8963.

Parador de Málaga-Gibralfaro (Map C–C1)
Views from Gibralfaro hill in the Alcazaba. Rustic building; part of the *parador* chain. ✉ S/N 29016 Málaga, ☎ 95 222 1902, ℡ 95 222 1904.

• MID-RANGE
Hotel Bahia de Málaga (Map C–A3)
Small, intimate, with convenient parking. ✉ Somera 8 – 29001 Málaga, ☎ 95 222 4305, ℡ 95 222 4303.

Hotel Los Naranjos
(Map I–A3)
Small hotel in a lively area, near Gibralfaro. ✉ Paseo de Sancha, 35 – 29016 Málaga, ☎ 95 222 4317, ℡ 95 222 5975.

• BUDGET
Hotel del Sur
(Map C–B3)
Quiet hotel south of Alameda gardens. ✉ Trinidad Grund 13, Málaga, ☎ 95 222 4803, ℡ 95 221 2416.

Niza (Map C–B2)
One-star; located in a main shopping street. ✉ Larios 2, Málaga, ☎ 95 222 7704.

Marbella and Surrounds
• LUXURY
Byblos Andaluz
(Map A–C2)
Deluxe hotel, health spa, fine restaurant. ✉ Urbanizacion Mijas Golf, Málaga, ☎ 95 246 0250, ℡ 95 247 6783.

Hotel Puente Romano (Map A–B3)
Jetset resort hotel. ✉ Ctra. Nac. 340, km 178, 29600 Marbella, ☎ 95 277 0100, ℡ 95 277 5766.

Marbella Club
(Map A–B3)
Andalucían/Moroccan style in gardens on Marbella's Golden Mile. ✉ Blvd. Principe Alfonso de Hohen-lohe, S/N, ☎ 95 282 2211, ℡ 95 282 9884.

• MID-RANGE
Hotel Mijas
(Map A–D2)
Comfortable three-star, lovely views. ✉ Urb. Tamisa S/N, 29650 Mijas, ☎ 95 248 5800, ℡ 95 248 5825.

La Fonda de Benalmádena
(Map A–D2)
Pretty, 26-room Andalucían-style hotel. ✉ c/Santo Domingo 7, Benalmádena Pueblo, ☎ and ℡ 95 256 8273.

Refúgio de Juanar
(Map A–A2)
Lodge in nature reserve near Marbella; serves game dishes. ✉ Sierra Blanca, 29610 Ojén, Málaga, ☎ and ℡ 95 288 1001.

• BUDGET
Hostal Enrequita
(Map A–B3)
Two-star town house near the old quarter. ✉ 29600 Marbella, ☎ 95 282 7552.

Miami (Map A–E2)
Hotel built around
an old mansion.
✉ Aladino 14, 29620
Torremolinos, Málaga,
☎ 95 238 5255.

Nerja
• LUXURY
Monica (Map I–C3)
Modern four-star with
good facilities.
✉ Playa Torrecilla,
29780 Nerja, ☎ 95 252
1100, 📠 95 252 1162.

Parador de Nerja
(Map I–C3)
Just outside town, lush
garden, view from cliff.
✉ Alumuñécar 8,
29780 Nerja, ☎ 95 252
0050, 📠 95 252 1997.

• MID-RANGE
**Hotel Balcón de
Europa** (Map I–C3)
Arguably the best in
town; lift to the beach.
✉ Balcón de Europa
1, 29780, ☎ 95 252
0800, 📠 95 252 4490.

• BUDGET
Hostal Avalon
(Map I–C3)
Tiny, near the beach.
✉ Punta Lara, 29780
Nerja, ☎ 95 252 0698.

Portofino (Map I–C3)
Small beach hotel,
central location.
✉ Puerto del Mar 2,
☎ 95 252 0150.

Ronda
• LUXURY
**Hotel Reina
Victoria** (Map K–A3)
Turn-of-the-century
hotel; sweeping views.
✉ c/Jerez 25, 29400
Ronda, ☎ 95 287
1240, 📠 95 287 1075.

Parador de Ronda
(Map K–B2)
Views over Tajo Gorge.
Rustic Andalucian cui-
sine, including game.
✉ Plaza de España
S/N, 29400, ☎ 95 287
7500, 📠 95 287 8188.

• MID-RANGE
El Tajo (Map K–A2)
Comfortable three-star
in Mercadillo section.
✉ c/Doctor Cajal 7,
29400, ☎ 95 287
4040, 📠 95 287 5099.

Polo (Map K–A2)
Three-star near the
bullring and gorge.
✉ c/Mariano Soubirón
8, 29400, ☎ 95 287
2447, 📠 95 287 2449.

• BUDGET
**Hotel Virgen de los
Reyes** (Map K–A2)
Close to the bullring.
All the rooms have
private bathrooms.
✉ c/Lorenzo Borrego
13, 29400 Ronda,
☎ 95 287 1140.

Sevilla
• LUXURY
Alcora (Map D–B2)
A modern four-star
hotel, located just
outside the centre.
✉ Ctra. San Juan-
Tomares, 41920 San
Juan Aznalfarache,
☎ 95 476 9400,
📠 95 417 0128.

Hotel Alfonso XIII
(Map E–A2)
Palatial, five-star Gran
Luxe hotel, where
royals stay.
✉ San Fernando 2,
41004, ☎ 95 422
2862, 📠 95 421 6033.

Hotel Doña María
(Map E–B2)
A charming hotel,
near the cathedral.
✉ c/Don Remondo
19, 41004,
☎ 95 422 4990,
📠 95 421 9546.

Hotel Tryp Colón

(Map E–B1)

Mock-Regency hotel, used by bullfighters.

✉ c/Canalejas 1, 41001, ☎ 95 422 2900, 📞 95 422 0938.

• MID-RANGE
Casas de la Juderia

(Map E–B2)

Houses converted into elegant apartments.

✉ callejon de Dos Fermanas 7, Plaza Santa María la Blanca, ☎ 95 441 5150, 📞 95 422 2170.

• BUDGET
Hostal Plaza-Sevilla

(Map E–B1)

Designed by architect of Plaza España.

✉ c/Canalejas 2, ☎ 95 421 7149, 📞 95 421 0773.

Sierra Nevada

• LUXURY
Hotel Melia Sierra Nevada (Map I–E1)

Modern hotel in the centre of ski resort.

✉ Pradollano S/N, 18196 Sierra Nevada, ☎ 95 848 0400, 📞 95 848 0458.

• MID-RANGE
Parador Nacional Sierra Nevada

(Map I–E1)

Above Pradollano, overlooks ski slopes.

✉ Ctra. Sierra Nevada km35, 18196 Sierra Nevada, ☎ 95 848 0200, 📞 95 848 0212.

• BUDGET
Hotel Telecabina

(Map I–E1)

One-star ski lodge, near the lift station.

✉ Plaza de Pradollano, 18196 Sierra Nevada, ☎ 95 828 9120, 📞 95 824 9140.

Tarifa

• LUXURY
Hotel Balcón de España (Map D–C6)

Just out of town, with pool and horse riding. Summer only.

✉ Ctra. Nac. 340, km77, ☎ 95 668 4326, 📞 95 668 0472.

• MID-RANGE
Hurricane Hotel

(Map D–C6)

Relaxed atmosphere; attracts windsurfers.

✉ Ctra. Nac. 340, km77, ☎ 95 668 4919.

White Towns

• LUXURY
Parador de Arcos de la Frontera

(Map D–B4)

On the main square; stunning views.

✉ Plaza del Cabildo S/N, 11630 Arcos de la Frontera, ☎ 95 670 0500, 📞 95 670 1116.

• MID-RANGE
Hotel el Convento

(Map D–B4)

A family-run hotel in an old convent, with a restaurant.

✉ c/Maldonado 2, 11630 Arcos de la Frontera, ☎ 95 670 0233.

Hotel el Molino del Santo (Map D–C4)

Converted mill with rustic furnishing.

✉ Bda. de la Estación, 29370 Benaoján, ☎ and 📞 95 216 7151.

Hotel Los Olivos

(Map D–B4)

Town house with a pretty patio.

✉ c/San Miguel 2, 11630 Arcos de la Frontera, ☎ 95 670 0811, 📞 95 670 2018.

EATING OUT
Food and Drink

Andalucían cuisine is tremendously varied, ranging from fresh seafood and colourful vegetable dishes to rich, meaty stews from the mountains. Preparation is relatively simple and flavours are strong, with widespread use of garlic, cumin (which has been around since the Moors lived in Andalucía), extra virgin olive oil and spicy marinades.

Tapas

The tapas bar has turned out to be one of Spain's most popular exports in recent years. This habit of consuming several small dishes with a glass of *fino*, the pale, dry sherry from Jerez, before dinner is an essential part of the Spanish working day. Because of the heat, Spaniards enjoy a long, late lunch followed by a *siesta* (rest) and work quite late into the evening. It is then customary to go for a stroll and have a few drinks accompanied by enough tapas to stave off any hunger until supper, which is usually as late as 22:00.

Right: *Tapas are served as snacks, but they can often be filling enough to constitute a meal.*

'Tapa' actually means 'lid' and its origin is the little plates of **snacks** bartenders used to place over the drinks. Some bars, those usually frequented most by the locals, serve free tapas at the bar, often something simple like bowls of **olives**, slices of *jamón serrano* (cured mountain ham) and plates of lightly **salted almonds**.

Elsewhere, a selection of tapas dishes is enough for an evening meal for most people. Specialities of the Costa del Sol include *pescaito frito* (small fish fried in batter), spicy *chorizo* sausages, *champiñones al ajillo* (mushrooms baked in garlic), *queso* (cubes of smoked cheese), red peppers in olive oil, and *tortilla* (Spanish omelette filled with potato and onion and served cold in slices).

Look out for *calamares* (tiny, marinated squid) and *canaillas* (miniature sea snails), which are regarded as a great delicacy. Offal is popular in this part of the world and small pieces of liver cooked with onion and spices is another favourite. All this should be washed down by a glass of chilled *fino*.

Regional Specialities

Andalucía is the home of *gazpacho*, a thick, cold soup made from tomatoes, onions, bread, cumin, lemon juice and vast quantities of fresh garlic. Usually served with diced green pepper, chopped hard-boiled egg and fried croutons, *gazpacho* is a meal in itself.

Another traditional **cold soup**, originating from Málaga and perfect for summer, is *ajo blanco*, made with almonds and garlic and served chilled with fresh grapes. When the weather is cooler, try *sopa de*

Common Culinary Terms

a la plancha – grilled
al ajillo – in garlic
asado – roast or barbecued
astofado – stewed
a la marinera – cooked in wine with garlic and parsley
al horno – baked
frito – fried
pescados – fish
mariscos – seafood
revueltos, or *huevos revueltos* – scrambled eggs, often served with asparagus, mushrooms or ham

---

Olives

Andalucians take pride in their olives because of the superior fruit yielded by the trees in southern Spain, and the special dressing which gives the olives their unique flavour. Cumin, marjoram, rosemary, thyme, bay leaf, garlic, savory and fennel are all used. Several types of olive are served as tapas: *aceituna de la reina*, the Queen's olive and the most prized; *aceituna gorda*, the 'fat olive'; *manzanilla*, a fine, dry flavoured fruit; and the black olive, known as the 'pearl of the Guadalquivir', grown around Sevilla.

Cheese

Traditionally eaten as a *tapa*, cheese occasionally appears at the end of meals accompanied by quince jelly. Most of the local cheeses are made of goat's milk – sometimes blended with sheep's milk – and do not travel well. This is why they are not exported. Look out for the fresh, cylindrical goat's cheese of the Alpujarras and Sierra Nevada and the stronger, yellow Ronda cheese, preserved in olive oil. Grazalema produces a unique sheep's cheese, cured for several months and preserved in vats of olive oil. *Queso de Cádiz* is a general term for the semi-cured goat's cheese from the mountains, yellow in colour and quite strong to taste. *Valle de los Pedrojes* is a sheep's cheese from around Córdoba. One of the most popular cheeses, hard, tangy *Manchego*, comes from La Mancha.

pescado, an all-encompassing term for **fish soup**, which is usually seasoned with tomato, onion, garlic and brandy.

Fish, not surprisingly, is the principal speciality of the coast. On some beaches, fishermen still cook fresh sardines on skewers over an open fire. In restaurants, fish is served marinated or fried, ranging from *calamares en su tinta* – tiny squid cooked in their own ink – to *gambas con ajillo*, giant prawns in garlic. Look out for *pez espada* (swordfish), *rape* (monkfish) and *bonito* (tuna), all of which are caught locally and served grilled, brushed with olive oil and seasoning.

Inland, traditional dishes incorporate the **game, freshwater fish** and **wild herbs** of the mountains. Casseroles are prepared using **rabbit** or **hare** cooked in white wine and a speciality of the Cádiz region, west of the Costa del Sol, is *pastel de pichones*, or **pigeon pâté**. In the Alpujarras in Granada province, a speciality is mountain **trout** stuffed with cured ham. One of the most widespread meat dishes is *rabo de torro* – **oxtail** prepared with tomatoes, onions and spices. Some of the recipes are not for the squeamish, particularly in the area around Granada where brains, intestines and bulls' testicles form the basis of a couple of specialities, *tortilla Sacromonte* and *revoltillos*.

Vegetarians will not starve, however, because the salads in Andalucía are quite delicious. They are generally made from crisp lettuce, succulent olives and huge, sweet tomatoes drizzled with olive oil, with a number of variations in ingredients including artichoke, fresh asparagus and chopped eggs. Vegetable dishes that can

be found in several of the restaurants of the region include *espinaces con ajillo* (spinach with garlic), *garbanzos con espinaces* (chickpeas with spinach) and *judías verdes con salsa de tomate* (green beans with tomato sauce and fresh garlic).

Above: *Sardines roasted on skewers in the sand are a typical sight on the beaches of Torremolinos.*

Sherry

Andalucía's most famous wine comes from a small area around the town of **Jerez de la Frontera,** which forms one corner of the 'sherry triangle' with El Puerto de Santa María and Sanlúcar de Barrameda in the province of Cádiz, a couple of hours' drive inland from the Costa del Sol. The climate, salty sea air, chalky soil and generations of expertise produces the world's finest *fino,* the dry, pale gold sherry drunk chilled all over Andalucía with tapas.

The name 'sherry' is an anglicized version of the name of the town **Jerez,** which in turn is a corruption of the Moorish name *Xerez.* The Phoenicians were the original wine-growers in the area, followed by the Romans, who exported wine from Jerez all

Andalucían Imports
Many of the ingredients that make up the gastronomic specialities of southern Spain are not native to the region. Phocian Greeks brought **olives** and **vines** around 1000BC and the Moors, hundreds of years later, introduced **pepper, cumin, cinnamon** and **coriander**. The conquering of the Americas brought hitherto unknown foods such as **maize, potatoes, tomatoes** and, of course, **tobacco**.

Right: *Sherry is presented with a flourish at tastings in the* bodegas.

over their empire. After the *reconquista* drove out the Moors and Jews, British firms established *bodegas* (wine cellars) in the area and to this day, Britain remains the biggest export market, consuming some 70% of all sherry exported from Spain.

In addition to *fino*, there are three other types of sherry drunk in Spain. *Manzanilla* is a type of dry *fino* with a salty tang, acquired from the area around Sanlúcar de Barrameda and a perfect accompaniment to the seafood in which the area specializes. *Amontillado*, meanwhile, is a more pungent wine that has been aged beyond its normal span in the *bodega*, while *Oloroso*, the heaviest style of sherry, is usually sweetened and sold as cream exclusively to the British market.

Wine

Most of Spain's famous wine-producing areas are in the north but the area immediately behind the Costa del Sol does grow some wine of its own. Málaga has its own *Denominacion de Origen* growing mainly **Moscatel** and **Pedro Ximenez** grapes producing dark, sweet wines.

Wine in supermarkets and restaurants along the Costa del Sol is exceptionally good value and while they may not be local, names to look out for include **Campo Viejo** (fruity reds and dry whites), **Marqués de Caceres** (red *Riojas* and oak-aged whites) and **Torres** (fruity, aromatic whites like Viña Sol and Esmerelda and soft, fresh reds). *Cava* is sparkling wine made using the champagne method and the two biggest producers are **Codorníu** and **Freixenet**. Andalucía is also Spain's biggest brandy producer, mainly from the sherry *bodegas* around Jerez.

One drink that every visitor to the Costa del Sol is likely to encounter is *sangria*, a marvellous concoction of chilled red wine, citrus fruits, lemonade, brandy and ice, which is drunk by Spaniards at barbecues and picnics. *Sangria* is very refreshing and its easy, drinkable quality means that some tourists consume it to excess, underestimating its potency.

Where to Eat

The Costa del Sol has various different types of eating establishments. **Tapas** bars, *tascas*, **bodegas**, *cervecerias* and **tabernas** are all types of bars serving food. A *comedor* is a simple dining room, usually attached to a bar, and a *venta* is a similar setup in the countryside, usually with a small shop as well. Restaurants are graded from one to five forks, but this relates to price rather than quality. A *marisqueria* restaurant specializes in seafood and an *asado* in barbecued food.

Tipping

Spaniards are relaxed about tipping etiquette. A **service charge** is always included in hotel bills and sometimes in restaurant bills. If not included, **10%** of the total is appropriate. Taxi drivers and bartenders will also be happy with 10%. Many filling stations are not self-service, in which case you should tip the attendant up to 100 pesetas. The same applies to hotel porters and bullfight ushers.

Rum

A surprising fact about the **Costa del Sol** is that it introduced rum to the **West Indies**. The only sugar cane grown in Europe comes from **Málaga** and **Granada** provinces and it was from here that the cane, which is not native to the West Indies, and its distilling techniques were taken to the New World in the 16th century. Rum is still produced in Spain today, in **Cádiz** and around **Motril**, in **Granada** province.

Almuñécar
Casa Paco
Rather expensive but excellent seafood; the custard apple tart is the house speciality.
✉ *Playa Velilla seafront,* ☎ *95 628 5451.*

Antequera
La Espuela
An atmospheric restaurant built inside the bullring. Creative fish and vegetables. Try *rabo de toro*, the house speciality.
✉ *Paseo Maria Cristina S/N, Plaza de Toros, 29200 Antequera,* ☎ *95 270 2633,* ✆ *95 284 0616.*

Benalmádena
Hotel Torrequebrada, Café Royal
Big casino complex with gourmet restaurant (*see page 75*).
✉ *Casino Torrequebrada, 29630 Benalmádena Costa,* ☎ *95 244 6000.*

Córdoba
Bar Sociedad de Plateros
A lively bar near the centre, serving great tapas. Good value for money.
✉ *San Francisco 6, Córdoba.*

El Caballo Rojo
Andalucían with an Arab influence – try dishes such as lamb in honey and monkfish with pine nuts.
✉ *Cardenal Herrero 28, Córdoba,* ☎ *95 747 5375.*

Estepona and Surrounds
Bar Mesón El Cordobes
Good tapas bar, central, open until 22:00.
✉ *Plaza de las Flores 16, Estepona,* ☎ *95 280 0737.*

Cabo Mayor
For memorable gourmet dining, visit this restaurant.
✉ *Club Marítimo Hotel, Puerto Sotogrande,* ☎ *95 679 0390.*

El Carnicero
A friendly, rustic place just outside Estepona, specializing in Spanish country cooking.
✉ *La Cancelada, Ctra. Cádiz km165,* ☎ *95 278 5123.*

Mesón El Coto
Mountain setting near coast. Barbecues and game specialities.
✉ *El Madronal, Ctra. de Ronda,* ☎ *95 278 6688.*

Fuengirola
La Casa Vieja
Village house with patio; serves Spanish specialities.
✉ *Avenida de las Boliches 27, Las Boliches,* ☎ *95 258 3830.*

Gibraltar
Admiral Collingwood's
Serves traditional English food; offers a Sunday carvery.
✉ *The Square, Marina Bay,* ☎ *350 79 241.*

Bunter's Bar Restaurant
This is the place to go for reliable English and vegetarian dishes.
✉ *College Lane,* ☎ *350 70 482.*

Caleta Hotel
Romantic Italian restaurant within the hotel, serving home-made pasta.
✉ *Catalan Bay,*
☎ *350 76 501,*
✆ *350 42 143.*

La Bayuca
Gibraltar's oldest restaurant. Scottish beef and apple pie are the specialities.
✉ *21 Turnbulls Lane,*
☎ *350 75 119.*

Granada
La Alacena de las Monjas
Original Spanish cuisine is served in the vaults of this 15th-century convent.
✉ *Plaza Padre Suarez 5,* ☎ *95 822 4028.*

Mirador de Morayma
Mouthwatering Granada specialities in romantic old house with walled gardens and views of the magnificent Alhambra.
✉ *C7 Pianista Garcia Carrillo 2, Barrio de Albaicín,*
☎ *95 822 8290.*

Ruta del Veleta
Gourmet cooking in atmospheric restaurant 5km (3 miles) from the city on the Veleta road. Closed Sundays for dinner.
✉ *ctra. de Sierra Nevada, km5.4,*
☎ *95 848 6134.*

Jerez de la Frontera
El Abaco
Intimate restaurant in the hotel grounds, serves fresh seafood.
✉ *Avda. Alvaro domecq 11,* ☎ *95 630 3011,* ✆ *95 631 1300.*

La Mesa Redonda
Good value, extensive menu. Closed Sundays, holidays, and summer.
✉ *c/Manuel de la Quintana 3,*
☎ *95 634 0064.*

Las Alpujarras
Bar Frenfría
Next to a stream, great views, excellent regional specialities.
✉ *ctra. de la Sierra, 18412 Bubión, Granada,*
☎ *95 876 3234.*

Meson La Fragua
Popular with hikers, serves Alpujarrian food. It is closed every year from 10 January to 10 February.
✉ *c/San Antonio 4, Trevélez,*
☎ *95 885 8573.*

Málaga
Antigua Casa de Guardia
Local legend, serves seafood tapas to a lively crowd. Wine is served from wooden barrels behind the bar.
✉ *Alameda 18, Málaga,*
☎ *95 221 4680.*

Antonio Martin
Historic seafront restaurant specializing in fish. There is a terrace in summer; a log fire in winter.
✉ *Plaza de la Mala-guete, S/N,*
☎ *95 222 7382.*

Bar Lo Gueno
Lively bar/restaurant with a wide range of tapas and *raciónes*, hams and cheeses.
✉ *Marin Garcia 9, Málaga.*

El Cabra

This well-known seafood restaurant is situated right on the waterfront.

⊠ *C/Menita 20, Málaga,*
☎ *95 229 1595.*

Parador de Málaga-Gibralfaro

Creative game cooking in addition to excellent fish dishes, with romantic views of the city.

⊠ *S/N 29016 Málaga,*
☎ *95 222 1902,*
✆ *95 222 1904.*

Marbella
Albahaca

Largely vegetarian restaurant specializing in Andalucían and Galician dishes.

⊠ *calle Lobatas 31, Marbella,*
☎ *95 286 3520.*

Dalli's Pasta Factory

Popular pasta restaurant run by local chain, representing very good value in Puerto Banús.

⊠ *Puerto Banús,*
☎ *95 281 2490.*

El Portalón

High quality, traditional cooking on the Golden Mile.

⊠ *Carretera de Cádiz km178, Marbella,*
☎ *95 282 7880,*
✆ *95 286 1075.*

La Meridiana

Rated by *Spanish Gourmet* magazine as one of the best. It is closed at lunchtime.

⊠ *Camino de la Cruz, Marbella,*
☎ *95 277 6190.*

Marisquería La Pesquería

Fish restaurant in the old town serving excellent tapas.

⊠ *Plaza de la Victoria, 29600 Marbella,*
☎ *95 277 8054.*

Nerja
Bar el Mirador

Bar and barbecue at the top of Frigiliana village, with breathtaking views.

⊠ *Frigiliana.*

Casa Luque

An elegant old house in a clifftop location with lovely gardens. Serves local food and occasionally has flamenco dancing.

⊠ *Balcón de Europa, Nerja,* ☎ *95 252 1004.*

El Capricho

This rustic village restaurant inland from Almuñécar serves various local specialities, including chicken with apples and roast meats.

⊠ *c/Carretera, Otivar,*
☎ *95 864 5025.*

La Capilla del Mar

Popular restaurant specializing in game.

⊠ *c/de la Cruz 16, Nerja,* ☎ *95 252 1993.*

Meson Antonio

Tapas and *raciónes* are the specialities of this establishment.

⊠ *c/Diputación 18, Nerja,* ☎ *95 252 0033.*

Ronda
Don Miguel

Good, wholesome food and stunning location, built next to the Puente Nueve.

⊠ *Villanueva 4,*
☎ *95 287 1090.*

Parador de Ronda

Regional specialities in a dramatic setting.
⊠ Plaza de España S/N, 29400 Ronda,
☎ 95 287 7500,
℡ 95 287 8188.

Pedro Romero

Famous eatery with a bullfighting theme. Regional specialities.
⊠ Virgen de la Paz 16,
☎ 95 287 1110.

Restaurante Jerez

Meat dishes including rabo de torro (oxtail).
⊠ Plaza Teniente Arce 2, ☎ 95 287 9028.

Sevilla

La Albahaca

Expensive Andalucían restaurant; serves good fish and game. Closed on Sundays.
⊠ Plaza de Santa Cruz 12, Sevilla,
☎ 95 456 1204.

Meson Don Raimundo

Andalucían food served in a former convent. Closed Sunday dinner.
⊠ c/Argote de Molina 26, Sevilla,
☎ 95 422 3355.

El Rinconcillo

Founded in 1670, Sevilla's oldest bar is also one of its best. Good tapas range.
⊠ c/Gerona 40, Barrio Macarena.

The Triana district

Try the riverside tapas bars in the gypsy quarter along Betis Street.
⊠ Across the river from Plaza del Toros.

Tarifa

Hurricane Hotel

Original cuisine with plenty of salads and fish. Value for money.
⊠ Ctra. Nac. 340, km77, 11380 Tarifa,
☎ 95 668 4919.

Torremolinos

Casa Juan

Famous fish restaurant; great atmosphere and reasonable prices.
⊠ La Carihuela,
☎ 95 237 6523.

El Comedor

Basque specialities including seafood crépes and venison.
⊠ calle Casablanca S/N, Torremolinos,
☎ 95 238 2881.

White Towns

Casa de las Piedras

This restaurant serves many local specialities including asparagus with wild mushrooms and fresh trout stuffed with ham.
⊠ c/Las Piedras, Grazalema,
☎ 95 613 2014.

Hostal Las Truchas

Rustic hostel, peaceful location. Try the trout stuffed with jamón serrano (cured ham).
⊠ Avenida de Cádiz 1, 11670 El Bosque,
☎ 95 671 6061.

Parador de Arcos de la Frontera

The restaurant has menu degustación, with nine or ten small courses of local dishes.
⊠ Plaza del Cabildo S/N, 11630 Arcos de la Frontera, ☎ 95 670 0500, ℡ 95 670 1116.

Restaurante el Convento

Local specialities in an atmospheric setting.
⊠ c/Marqués de Torresoto 7.

ENTERTAINMENT
Bullfighting

The bullfight, also known as the **Fiesta Brava**, **Los Toros** or **La Lidia**, is an ancient art steeped in ritual and is recorded as far back as 2000BC, in a wall painting excavated at Knossós in Crete depicting acrobats vaulting over a charging bull. The Visigoths who once inhabited Andalucía practised a primitive form of bullfighting but it was the Moors, almost 3000 years later, who turned the spectacle into an art form. It became more widespread in the late 18th century.

Love it or hate it, a *corrida* (bullfight) provides a valuable insight into the culture of Andalucía. The real stars of the ring can be seen in Sevilla and Córdoba, although Málaga, Estepona and Marbella all attract a knowledgeable and enthusiastic following.

A typical *corrida* involves three matadors and six bulls, massive fighting specimens which have been specially bred for their aggression. Each encounter will last about 15 minutes and forms three acts. The star of the show is the matador, expensively dressed in a *traje de lucas* (suit of lights), consisting of an intricately embroidered silk jacket, black pants and a *montera*, or bicorne hat.

First, the bull is taunted by *banderilleros* with magenta capes swept in graceful arcs, before the *picadores* enter the ring mounted on horseback. Their job is to lance the bull's neck and weaken its muscles in preparation for the kill. Next, the *banderilleros*, who are on foot, drive brightly coloured steel darts into the bull's shoulders before the matador is finally alone in the ring with the bull for the final act, the *faena* or *la suerte de la muerte* (*muerte* means death). The matador works the crowd into a frenzy as he plays with the maddened bull using a small cape before moving in for the kill, in which he plunges his sword between the animal's shoulder blades. Matadors are national heroes and some become millionaires, but most of them incur serious wounds during their careers and many pay with their lives.

Flamenco

Impromptu flamenco under the stars on a hot summer's night, or in a smoky bar in the backstreets of Málaga is a primitive, magical experience which is far removed from the frills and castanets of the 'typical folklore' promoted in the tourist resorts.

Essentially an outlet for passion and unhappiness, good flamenco is a spiritual bond between musicians, dancers and onlookers. As the raw emotion of the song, the hypnotic hand-clapping and finger-snapping of the audience and the amazingly fast stamping of the dancer build up to a cathartic finale, it is accompanied by spontaneous shouts of encouragement and emotion.

Strands of many cultures have come together to form the music but it originates from the gypsies of **Sevilla**, **Jerez** and **Cádiz** in the 19th century who sang mournful laments of lost love and oppression. Elements of the music come from **North Africa**, **India**, **Greece**, **Egypt** and **Pakistan**, but the result is pure Andalucía.

Bullfighting Overseas
Spain is not the only bullfighting country. **Mexico** stages regular *corridas* in winter, while **Peru** has its season in the autumn. Bullfights also take place in **Venezuela**, **Columbia** and **southern France** on feast days. **Portugal** has a bullfighting following as enthusiastic as Spain's, although the bull is not killed in front of the spectators, but in the slaughterhouse afterwards. The Spanish do not count Portugal as a bullfighting nation.

Opposite: Corridas *are a major attraction in Spain.*
Below: *The 'real' flamenco is worth seeking out.*

Tunas
If you are serenaded in a restaurant by a group of young men dressed in balloon breeches and long black stockings, don't be surprised. These are **tunas** – students from Málaga University keeping alive an ancient tradition and earning their drinking money at the same time. They perform popular and classic Spanish songs on the guitar, mandolin, violin and using castanets.
Under Alfonso the Wise in the 12th century, begging was prohibited but poor students were allowed to sing and play for their supper as *tunas*, wearing a coloured armband to distinguish them from the beggars.

Below: *Colourful costumes are worn in traditional flamenco dancing.*

Flamenco became part of civilized society in the 19th century, and also began to be integrated into popular folklore music. The *sevillana* is one of the most popular forms, celebrated at Andalucía's many summer festivals and popular among young people, most of whom know the basic steps. This is the only form of flamenco where castanets are used, contrary to popular belief, and elsewhere visitors are expected to join in with *palmadas* (hand clapping) and *pitos* (finger snapping) to create the staccato counter-rhythms to the drumming of the dancer's feet. Male roles have more emphasis on footwork, while the female dancers demonstrate body and hand movements that are both dramatic and graceful. Their brilliantly coloured dresses are cut higher at the front to show off the skill in the steps.

Flamenco is used to express joy as well as agony and there are three levels of intensity: *grande* or *jondo* (deep); *intermedio*, which is much less profound and sometimes sounds almost oriental; and *pequeno* or

canto chico, a lighter, more joyful form of flamenco. The dances include the *tango*, *fandango*, *farruca* and *zambra*, although everything is improvised within a repertoire of fixed rhythms. A point to note is that the guitarist follows the dancer, not the other way round, and *duende*, which is the moment of total understanding between the musician, the dancer and the *aficionados*, is achieved when the three are completely immersed in the music and dance.

The visitor's best chance of finding some good traditional flamenco is to join in with a local *feria*, where talented travelling artistes often perform. The local tourist office will be able give some advice on the best *café cantantes*, where flamenco is performed; most are located in the backstreets of Málaga and Sevilla.

Music and Theatre

There are a number of music and theatre venues in the Costa del Sol. In **Málaga**, Teatro Cervantes puts on international standard theatre, dance and music. The Salón Varietes Theatre in **Fuengirola** is an English-speaking theatre offering various productions from October to May, including musicals, plays and sometimes concerts too.

In **Sevilla**, Teatro de la Maestranza, situated near the bullring, is a theatre and opera house complex with seating for 1800. Regular performances by top international companies are offered here. Also in Sevilla is the beautiful Teatro Lope de Vega. Dating from 1929 and originally a casino, this neo-Baroque theatre still has regular exhibitions and performances. (For more theatres, *see* panel, right.)

Teatro Cervantes
⊠ c/Ramon Marin S/N, Málaga,
☎ 95 222 4109.

Salón Varietes Theatre
⊠ c/Emancipación, Fuengirola,
☎ 95 247 4542.

Teatro de la Maestranza
⊠ Paseo de Cristóbal Colon 22, Sevilla,
☎ 95 422 6573.

Teatro Lope de Vega
⊠ Avenida Maria Luisa S/N, Sevilla,
☎ 95 459 0853.

El Auditorio
⊠ Camino del Descubrimiento S/N, Isla de la Cartuja, Sevilla,
☎ 95 446 0748.

Córdoba Conservatorio Superior de Musica
⊠ c/Angel de Saavedra 1, Córdoba,
☎ 95 747 3909.

Municipal Theatre
⊠ El Ejido, Almería,
☎ 95 054 1007.

Above: *The Barqueta Bridge in Sevilla is brightly lit at night.*

Nightlife

Nightlife on the Costa del Sol tends to get going late, with most clubs empty until after midnight. **Torremolinos** has the biggest variety, with everything from high-tech discos to drag shows in the neon-lit **Calle San Miguel**. **Benalmádena** is quieter but by no means tame, the **Arroyo de la Miel** being the area most frequented by locals.

Marbella nightlife is generally more upmarket than anywhere else, with several expensive clubs and cocktail lounges. Around **Puerto Banús**, the entertainment caters to every taste and the whole port buzzes with partygoers and clubbers until dawn during the summer months.

Málaga's best tapas bars are clustered in the streets around the cathedral and north of the Alameda (park). These are the places to try the sweet Málaga wine and fried fish, the local speciality – assorted seafood caught the same day and tossed in a deliciously light batter and deep fried. The atmospheric Antigua Casa on the Alameda is lined with barrels of sweet wine and is a popular place with the locals for a glass of *fino* and some shellfish tapas.

Gambling

There are two casinos on the Costa del Sol: one at the Hotel Torrequebrada on the coast outside Benalmádena, and a second at Puerto Banús in the Hotel Andalucía Plaza.

Casino Torrequebrada is a big casino complex which offers a variety of games – both French and American roulette, blackjack, as well as slot machines. It also has private gaming rooms, a piano bar and a gourmet restaurant. *La Fortuna* is a cabaret with flamenco shows. The casino is situated inside the Hotel Torrequebrada, which has facilities for conferences as well as an excellent 18-hole golf course.

Casino Nueva Andalucía, part of the Andalucía Plaza Hotel, is a huge casino that also produces live shows during the summer months. Games on offer at this venue include roulette, baccarat, chemin de fer, craps, blackjack and poker, and in addition there are approximately 70 slot machines. The complex has a lively bar, a nightclub (**La Caseta del Casino**) and a private gaming area. You must be over 18 years old to get into the casino, and you will need to bring your identity document or passport for identification.

For casual gamblers who aren't really interested in going to a casino, the Spanish lottery is very popular – tickets are obtainable from any *lotería*. The results of the lottery are published in most newspapers on the day after the draw. On 22 December each year, **El Gordo** (the fat one) takes place. As its name suggests, this is the biggest lottery draw of the year and the whole of Spain usually stops work to listen to the result.

Carratraca

Some 5km (3 miles) from Ardales, the tiny village of Carratraca found fame in the 19th century as royalty and famous names, among them Lord Byron and Alexander Dumas, came from afar to take the waters and gamble in the three **casinos**. The foul-smelling **sulphur baths** are still open between June and October, although the casinos have been replaced by cafés.

Casino Torrequebrada

✉ Carretera Cadiz/Málaga km.220, Benalmádena,
☎ 95 244 6000,
🖥 www.infotu.com/malingle/becasino.htm
🕐 open daily 20:00–04:00.

Casino Nueva Andalucía

✉ Puerto de Banús, Apdo 21, Marbella, Málaga, 29600,
☎ 95 281 4000,
📠 95 281 2844,
🖥 www.casinocity.com/es/malaga/esandalu/
🖥 www.marbella2000.com/
🕐 open Mon–Thu 20:00–04:00, Fri–Sat 20:00–05:00.

Below: *Golfers are spoilt for choice with over 40 courses.*

Spectator Sports

Golf

Atalaya Golf and Country Club

One of the oldest golf courses in Andalucía.
✉ *Ctra de Benahavis, Km 0.7, Estepona,*
☎ *95 288 2812,*
✆ *95 288 7897,*
✉ *atalaya@golf-andalucia.net*

Club de Golf Valderrama

This course hosted the 1997 Ryder Cup.
✉ *Avda de los Cortijos S/N, Sotogrande,* ☎ *95 679 1200,* ✆ *95 679 6028,*
✉ *themanager@valderrama.com*
🖥 *www.golfspain.com*

Mijas Golf Club

Large 36-hole course.
✉ *Apartado 145, Urbanizacion Mijas Golf, Fuengirola,*
☎ *95 247 6843,*
✆ *95 246 7943.*

Tennis

Marbella Hill Tennis Club, ✉ *Avenida El Fuerte, Marbella,*
☎ *95 286 1500.*

Manolo Santana Racquets Club

✉ *Ctra de Istan km 2, Marbella,* ☎ *95 277 8580,* ✆ *95 286 5487,*
✉ *racquetsclub@royalwd.com*

Cricket

Marbella Cricket Club, ☎ *95 248 5629.*

Bars and Nightclubs

Cafe Rock Irlandes

A lively Irish pub.
✉ c/Realenga de San Luis 11, Málaga,
☎ 95 236 2182.

Cheers Café Bar

American-style bar, opposite cathedral.
✉ Plaza del Obispo 1, Málaga.

Colon

A typical tapas bar.
✉ c/Alameda de Colón 22, Málaga,
☎ 95 222 2103.

La Botica

Good choice of tapas.
✉ c/Pasaje Aralar 4, Málaga,
☎ 95 239 6489.

O'Neill's Pub

Another Irish pub.
✉ c/Luis de Velazquez 3, Málaga, ☎ 95 260 1460.

Tablao Flamenco Vista Andalucia

Traditional Andalucían bar.
✉ Avenida de Los Guindos S/N, Málaga,
☎ 95 223 1157.

Cafeteria Molino

A tapas bar serving good, plain fare.
✉ c/Alonso Bazan, Marbella,
☎ 95 282 3188.

Cerveceria Gambrinus

Excellent seafood tapas. Slightly above-average prices, but well worth it.
✉ c/Ramon Gomez de la Serna, Marbella, ☎ 95 286 3572.

Deep

This nightclub features the best international DJs.
✉ Ctra de Cadiz km 192, Hotel Don Carlos, Marbella.

Be Maná

The latest European dance music in lively surroundings; entry fee at weekends.
✉ Puerto Marina, Benalmadena Costa.

Caché

Bar and nightclub with free entry, open 21:00 till late.
✉ Puerto Marina, Benalmadena Costa.

Gay Spain

Homosexuality was made legal in Spain in 1978 and the age of consent is 18. Torremolinos is the gay centre on the coast, although the scene here is unobtrusive to straight visitors and some of the drag bars along the **Calle San Miguel** attract a huge, mixed following. Sevilla also has a large resident gay population. A good guide to gay life in Spain is **Spartacus España**, available in the UK and the USA.

EXCURSIONS
Morocco

Travel agents sell shopping trips to **Tangier** in Morocco and to a lesser extent, to **Ceuta**, one of two tiny enclaves of Spanish territory in **North Africa**. While Tangier can in no way be compared with the beautiful imperial cities of **Fez** and **Marrakech** further south, it still provides a brief taste of Morocco and a good opportunity for shopping in the market.

Ferries make the 2½-hour crossing from **Algeciras**, a busy port west of Gibraltar, several times a day. An important strategic point, guarding the entrance to the Mediterranean like Gibraltar, **Tangier** has been occupied by Greeks, Phoenicians, Vandals, Arabs, Berbers, Almoravids, Almohads, Spanish, Portuguese, British and French. Not surprisingly then, a number of different influences in the architecture are noticeable, although the medina, the old town by the port, is distinctly Arabic.

The narrow streets around Grand Socco Square are a great place to bargain for carpets, leather bags and jackets, brassware, herbs, spices and wooden carvings. Visitors may not enter mosques, although the **Dar el-Makhzen Palace** (⊕ Wed–Mon 09:00–13:00 and 15:00–18:00) houses excellent museums of Moroccan art and antiquities.

The biggest attraction of **Ceuta**, a Spanish colony 1½ hours from Algeciras by ferry, is its tax- and duty-free status, hence the large number of shops.

Shopping in Morocco

Haggling is a way of life in Morocco and should be considered part of the culture, not a threat or an insult to visitors. First, decide what you think an item is worth after shopping around. Expect to pay about one fifth of the 'official' price but start lower and prepare to meet in the middle. Be polite but firm. Vendors will try every trick – expressions of disbelief, stories of hardship – but don't be fooled. Some will offer mint tea, the traditional Arabic way of doing business, and if you are genuinely interested in making a purchase, it is polite to accept, but keep haggling. Sometimes it pays to shrug politely and walk away as a final tactic – if the vendor is still keen to sell, he will soon follow you with a lower offer.

Sevilla

Sevilla is packed with architectural treasures. Romans, Moors, Christians and modern man have all shaped the city's monuments, which include **La Giralda** (*see* page 23), the **Alcázar** (*see* page 24) and the **Cathedral** (*see* page 35).

East of the cathedral is the **Barrio Santa Cruz**, formerly the Jewish quarter until its residents were expelled in 1492. Today, the streets are full of tapas bars and restaurants, and open doors reveal glimpses of patios, shaded by greenery and cooled by a central fountain. A permanent art exhibition in the **Hospicio de los Venerables Sacerdotes**, a former hospice, is worth a visit.

Parque de María Luisa, the site of the 1929 Expo of the Americas, has magnificent pavilions representing the nations of the Americas. The highlight is the **Plaza de España**, a lavish building adorned with blue and white tiles. The semicircular design represents Spain welcoming the world with open arms, and the four bridges, the kingdoms of León, Castilla, Aragón and Navarra. Each of the ceramic pictures around the base depicts a province of Spain, complete with a map.

The 20th century has left his own mark on the city's architecture with **Expo '92**, a cluster of glassy pavilions on **La Isla de la Cartuja**, an island in the Guadalquivir River. Seven futuristic bridges linking the island to the city have become symbols of Sevilla and the former Expo site is now being developed as a theme park.

Sevilla
Location: Map E
Distance from
Málaga: 276km
(172 miles)

Sevilla Tourist Office
☎ 95 422 1404

Boat Rides on the Guadalquivir
✉ Boats depart from the wharf next to Torre del Oro.
🕐 every 30 minutes between 11:00 and 22:00
☎ 95 421 1396 or 456 1692

Opposite: *Day trips to Morocco are a shoppers' paradise.*
Below: *Sevilla's magnificent Giralda Tower is visible from miles around.*

EXCURSIONS

Córdoba
Location: Map B
Distance from
Málaga: 175km
(109 miles)

Municipal Tourist
Office
⊠ Plaza Judá Leví S/N,
☎ 95 720 0522,
📠 95 720 0277

Alcázar de los Reyes
Cristianos
⊠ Caballerizas Reales
S/N,
☎ 95 748 5001

Córdoba

Córdoba basks in the hot sun of the plains on the banks of the Guadalquivir, upstream from Sevilla. Founded in 152BC by the **Romans**, Córdoba later became the capital of Moorish Spain, a city of incredible wealth, learning and culture. From the 11th century, it was also a thriving **Jewish** community.

But Córdoba fell to the **Christians** in 1236, after which its glory faded. Plagues, battering by the French in the Napoleonic wars and even more suffering during the **Spanish Civil War** depleted the city. Now it exists as a prosperous regional centre, thanks to olive oil production and tourism.

Córdoba is essentially famous for one monument, **La Mezquita** (*see* page 26). The streets are a riot of colour in summer, scarlet and pink geraniums cascading from balconies. Northeast of the Mezquita, the **Callejón de los Flores** is one of the most beautiful.

Outside the mosque, the **Judería** is a fascinating tangle of narrow streets containing one of only three synagogues – this one built in 1315 – to survive the Christian reconquest of Andalucía. Nearby is a craft market and a bullfighting museum. Situated to the west of the Mezquita is the **Alcázar**, a fine 14th-century Mudéjar palace on the riverbank. The shady gardens look out over the old Roman bridge over the Guadalquivir River and an original Moorish waterwheel.

Below: *Córdoba's magnificent bridge, Puente Romano, is part of the city's Roman heritage.*

Granada

Granada boasts one of Andalucía's most exquisite Moorish palaces, the beautiful, red-walled **Alhambra** (*see* page 25). The temptation is to spend as long as possible admiring the palace, but there are other fascinating areas

of the city to explore; the **Generalife** (*see* page 40), the old silk market around the **Capilla Real** (*see* page 35) and the **Albaicín**, a cluster of narrow streets comprising the old Arab quarter.

Full of atmosphere, the Albaicín clings precariously to a hillside facing the Alhambra; most of the cobbled streets are too narrow for cars to negotiate. Iron grilles across the doors of the tiny white-washed houses reveal hidden *carmens*, or town gardens – exquisite patios bursting with vines, lemon trees and pomegranates, often with a fountain tinkling at the centre. From the **Mirador de la Morayma**, the highest point, the views of the Alhambra glowing red in the late afternoon sun are breathtaking. The little square is a place to sit and contemplate the view and listen to old gypsy women clicking castanets and humming arias from *Carmen*.

Outside the Alhambra, the hillside off the **Camino de Sacromonte** is dotted with natural cave openings, which until recently were inhabited by gypsies. The area is not particularly safe because of petty thievery and bag-snatching, but in daylight merits a brief stroll for the odd surprise.

Above: *Granada's Alhambra looks down on the rooftops and patios of the Albaicín (Arab) quarter.*

Granada
Location: Map G
Distance from Málaga: 127km (79 miles)

Tourist Information Office
✉ Plaza Mariana Pineda 10, 18009 Granada,
☎ 95 822 6688
📠 95 822 8916

Tourism Promotion Board
☎ 95 883 8378
📠 95 883 8379

Above: The high altitude of the Sierra Nevada makes it an ideal location for an observatory.

The Sierra Nevada

Spain's highest mountain range, the Sierra Nevada, stretches from east to west between Granada and the Costa del Sol. Rugged and remote, the high peaks of **Veleta** (3392m; 11,129ft) and **Mulhacén** (3481m; 11,421ft) are covered in snow for much of the year. On the north-facing slopes of Veleta is Europe's most southerly ski area, **Solynieve**. Pradollano, the village itself, is a purpose-built ski station, composed of modern buildings in a rather bleak setting, but excellent for a day's skiing in spring snow and hot sun.

Skiable terrain includes some 2500ha (6178 acres) of marked pistes in an open treeless bowl, with skiing up to 3000m (9843ft). Of the trails, 15 are graded easy, 16 intermediate and six difficult. Nineteen ski lifts whisk skiers up the mountain from the village. Everything from equipment to ski tuition can be arranged in the resort.

In July and August, the mountain road is passable by car, but hikers can walk the trail when the snow has cleared, starting from the *parador* outside the village. The views are breathtaking, with the Atlas Mountains of Morocco visible on a clear day.

Several outdoor activities are arranged in the village in summer: tennis, hang-gliding, mountain biking, horse-riding, paragliding and archery. Mountain bikers can try out some exciting terrain here; the Borreguiles gondola lift runs all summer, transporting bikes and riders to a network of marked trails, graded according to difficulty.

The Sierra Nevada
Location: Map I–E1
Distance from Málaga: about 120km (75 miles)

Tourist Office
☎ 95 848 0648
🖷 95 824 9122

Skiing Conditions Information
☎ 95 824 9119 or 848 0153

Reservations Centre
☎ 95 824 9111

Ski School
☎ 95 848 0168

Las Alpujarras

The southern slopes of the Sierra Nevada, a series of valleys known as Las Alpujarras, are a revelation; the air is astonishingly clean and the views are stunning.

The spa town of **Lanjarón** is one of the biggest mineral water producers in Spain, and the spa baths are thought to have curative powers. Lanjarón has Moorish origins and there is a ruined castle below the main, tree-lined Avenida de Andalucía.

Orgiva is a colourful market town. Good buys include rugs, baskets, pottery and cured mountain ham. It is also the last petrol stop before heading into the high Alpujarras.

In the foothills of Mulhacén is a gorge, **Poqueira**, with three tiny white villages perched on the terraces above: **Bubión**, **Pampaneira** and **Capileira**. The architecture is quite different here, built in the original style of the Berber tribes and only otherwise found in Morocco's Atlas Mountains.

Outdoor activities include hiking, mountain biking and horse riding. More extreme sports are parapenting (hang gliding with a parachute), mountain climbing and offroad 4X4 expeditions.

In the village of **Bubión** (*see* page 47) visits can be arranged to the Tibetan Monastery of al-Atalaya, the birthplace of Osel, one of the first Buddhist lamas (priests) in the west.

Trevélez, a further 14km (9 miles) up the mountain road, is the highest village in Spain and a well-known spot for *jamón serrano* – cured ham.

Las Alpujarras
Location: Map I–F2
Distance from Málaga: about 120km (75 miles)

Bubión Town Council
☎ 95 876 3032

Capileira Town Council
☎ 95 876 3400

Lanjarón Town Council
☎ 95 877 0002

Orgiva Town Council
☎ 95 878 4189

Pampaneira Town Council
☎ 95 876 3001

Trevélez Town Council
☎ 95 885 8501

Below: *Snow-capped peaks, steep terraced slopes and white villages characterize the Alpujarras.*

Above: *The best way to arrive in glamorous Puerto Banús is by boat.*

Gestures

Some gestures in the Spanish repertoire are self-explanatory, e.g. pursing the fingertips and kissing them means 'this is wonderful'. Others have obscure origins. The way to say 'Let's have a drink' is to make a fist with the thumb and little finger extended, imitating the action of drinking from a *bota* (a leather drinking bottle). If someone runs two fingers down their cheeks, it means 'I am poor', coming from '*me he quedado a dos velas*', or 'I am down to my last two candles'. A hand with the first and fourth fingers raised means that someone has been unfaithful, the fingers representing the horns of the devil which tempted the cuckold.

Best Times to Visit

Málaga receives visitors all year round, broadly split into golfers in winter and holiday-makers in summer. July to September is too hot for most people to enjoy walking in the city, and December to February can be cloudy. In spring – March to May – the city is at its greenest, as are the plains of Antequera and the national parks of El Torcal and Garganta del Chorro. From September to November, after the harvest, the countryside is usually rather dry and barren and consequently less photogenic. El Torcal is windy and snowy in winter; spring is the best time to enjoy the wildflowers. In **Marbella**, summer is the liveliest time and the height of the tourist season. Winters are mild and pleasant and most attractions are open, although places like Puerto Banús will not be so busy out of season. Peak season for golf in the **Western Costa del Sol**, where the most prestigious courses are located, is the winter months of January to April, and any visitor expecting to play should book well in advance. Summer, like anywhere else on the Costa del Sol, is hot and dry, so the best months for touring and sightseeing are March to June. Winters tend to be mild, although Gibraltar often has a misty cloud hanging over it in the cooler months. In the spring and early summer, the mountain scenery around **Ronda** is at its best. Between June and September, when the coast is at its hottest, the slightly cooler temperatures at higher altitudes can be a welcome relief, although the plains around Jerez and Arcos de la Frontera can be even hotter at this time. Winter is often cloudy with some rain and snow in the mountains. Unlike the western area, the **Eastern Costa del Sol** is largely seasonal and is at its most lively during the summer months. The season begins around May and extends to October, between which months most villages celebrate their annual festivals. **Granada** is busy throughout the year but is probably at its most beautiful in spring, when the Sierra Nevada forms a snowy backdrop. November is also a good month to visit, when the trees are changing colour, the air is clear and the first snows have fallen in the mountains. **Sevilla** is at its best in spring, although hotels are full around the time of Holy Week and the April Fair, both of which fall around Easter. In summer, the city is too hot to explore on foot, reaching 40°C (104°F) on occasion. **Córdoba** has a similar climate. In

winter, the **Sierra Nevada** is covered with snow and is only worth visiting from January to March for skiers – the high passes are blocked by snow. July and August are the best months for hiking, when it is possible to climb Veleta and Mulhacén, the highest peaks. The **Alpujarras** are lovely from late spring to November when the first snows fall, but nights are very cold outside summer.

Tourist Information

The Spanish Tourist Board has offices in the **United Kingdom** (London); the **USA** (Chicago, Los Angeles, Miami and New York); **Canada** (Toronto); **Australia** (Sydney) and most European countries. The **Costa del Sol** also has its own Promotion Board: **Patronato Provincial de Turismo**, ✉ Calle Compositor Lehmberg Ruiz, 3, 29007 Málaga, ☎ 95 228 8354, 📠 95 228 6042. The

Costa del Sol Tourist Board has a very useful website: 🖥 www. visitcostadelsol.com There are local tourist information offices in most towns and resorts, including **Antequera**, **Ronda**, **Benalmádena Costa**, **Estepona**, **Nerja**, **Torremolinos**, **Jerez**, **Fuengirola**, **Almería**, **Marbella**, **Granada**, **Córdoba** and **Sevilla**.

Entry Requirements

All visitors need a passport or in certain cases, an identity card. Citizens of **Andorra**, **Liechtenstein**, **Monaco**, **Switzerland** and countries within the **EU** need only present an identity card with the exception of the **UK** and **Denmark**, citizens of which need a passport. UK visitors must have a full 10-year passport as of 1995. **US**, **Canadian** and **Japanese** citizens require a passport but no visa. Visas are required by citizens of **Australia** and **New**

Zealand. All visitors can stay for a period of up to 90 days, after which time a residence permit is required. **UK** citizens can stay for up to six months before a residence permit is required.

Customs

The maximum allowance for duty-free items brought into Spain is as follows: one litre of spirits or two of fortified wine; two litres of wine and 200 cigarettes. When bought and duty paid in the EU, the amounts are 10 litres of spirits, 90 litres of wine and 110 litres of beer, for private consumption only. Duty-free sales within the EU were abolished in June 1999. Euro and foreign currency, banker's drafts and traveller's cheques can be imported and exported without being declared, although an upper limit applies. Spanish customs officials are generally polite and easy to negotiate with, but travellers coming in from Morocco are subject to stringent searches.

Health Requirements

No vaccinations are required to enter Spain and the only real health hazards are the occasional upset stomach and the sun, which is very strong during the **summer** months from **June** to **September**. Visitors travelling onwards to **Morocco** should have polio and typhoid boosters to be on the safe side, but it is essential to check the exact requirements with the Moroccan embassy beforehand. EU citizens qualify for free medical treatment on presentation of the appropriate form (the E111 for British citizens). Visitors from elsewhere should arrange their own travel and medical insurance.

Getting There

The Costa del Sol can be reached by air, rail, road and boat. **Málaga** is the principal port and airport.
By Air: Málaga and Sevilla both have modern airports served direct by **Iberia**, the national airline of Spain, from most European cities. Málaga, however, is the main gateway to the **Costa del Sol** and in summer gets very busy with charter flights. **Gibraltar** is a more convenient gateway from **London** to the western side of the Costa del Sol, served by regular flights with **GB Airways**, a subsidiary of British Airways. Passengers travelling through Gibraltar should note that its entry requirements are the same as for Great Britain. **Granada** also has a domestic airport with flights to **Madrid** and other Spanish cities and **Jerez** is served by **GB Airways** from the UK.

There is no airport tax on departure.
Iberia Airlines of Spain: for flight information as well as reservations: ☎ 95 213 6166.
GB Airways: ☎ 350 79 200.

By Rail: Rail travel can be confusing in Spain as there are several different types of services. A new high-speed train, **AVE**, links Madrid with Córdoba in just two hours, with a connection onwards to Málaga in four hours. Long-distance trains, **RENFE**, take eight hours from Madrid to Málaga and there are direct daily trains to Málaga and Granada from Barcelona. The local trains are called **Talgo** and they link Málaga with several regional towns of Andalucía throughout the day. The **Moto/Auto Express** service carries cars and motorbikes on the train and there are various saver passes for visitors using the railway network, but check before leaving home, as some of the deals are only available outside Spain.

By Car: Travellers bringing their own car and residing outside the Eu must have a **Green Card**, as third party insurance is compulsory. An international driving licence is required. Driving in Spain is on the right.

Car Hire: There are several car hire companies based at Málaga Airport and most have offices in the main resorts. Drivers must be over 21 with at least one year's experience. Never leave anything in a car, as vehicle crime is a problem. Cars can be hired in Gibraltar and taken to Spain, but must be returned to Gibraltar. Spanish rental cars may not be taken into Gibraltar; park at La Línea and walk across instead.
Avis: ✉ Cortina del Muelle, Málaga, ☎ 95 221 6627.

Calendar of Festivals

January: *Cabalgate de los Reyes Magos* (Three Kings Parade), Málaga – parades of floats, with sweets distributed to the children.
February: *Carnaval* – pre-Lenten festivity.
March: *Semana Santa* (Holy Week), Sevilla and Málaga – sombre, nightly candlelit processions during the week before Easter.
April: *Feria de Abril* (April Fair), Sevilla – bullfights, flamenco, equestrian events and street parties.
May: *Feria del Caballo* (Horse Fair), Jerez – the highlight of the equestrian year.
11 June: *Corpus Christi* – a national holiday with bullfights and fireworks.
16 July: *Virgen del Carmen* – processions of boats celebrate the patroness of fishermen.
9–19 August: *Feria de Málaga* (Fair of the South of Spain) – funfairs, circuses, bullfights, flamenco.
September: *Feria de Ronda* – highlight is the *corrida goyesca*, a costumed bullfight. *Fiesta de la Vindímia*, Jerez – flamenco, parades and horse events following the wine harvest.
October: *San Miguel* fiesta in Granada.

Road Signs
Aduana • customs
Autopista (de peaje)
• motorway/highway
(toll road)
Ceda el paso
• give way
Circunvalación • ring
road or bypass
Cruce peligroso •
dangerous crossroads
Despacio • slow
Desviación • diversion
Entrada • entrance
Obras • workmen
Prohibido adelantar
• no overtaking
Estacionamento pro-
hibido • no parking
Sin plomo
• unleaded petrol
Salida • exit
Salida de camiones
• lorry exit
Puesto de soccoro
• first-aid post

Al-Andalus Express
Spain's version of the
Orient Express, the
Al-Andalus Express
operates in May, June,
September and
October, departing
Sevilla once a week to
make a five-day tour of
Córdoba, **Granada**
and **Málaga**. The
accommodation on
board the train is com-
parable to a luxury
hotel and the price
includes guided tours
in each city, dinner and
accommodation on the
train, meals in exclusive
restaurants and excur-
sions to cultural events
in each city.

Hertz: ✉ Alameda de
Colón 17, Málaga,
☎ 95 222 5597.
Autos Lara: ✉ Calle
Salvador Allende S/N,
Torremolinos,
☎ 95 138 1800.
Information on road
conditions and other
general travel infor-
mation is available in
Spanish on the
Teleruta service,
☎ 91 535 2222.
Petrol stations are
plentiful, with leaded
and lead-free petrol
and diesel. Some are
self-service and some
have attendants.
By Boat: Ferries sail
to both **Melilla** and
Ceuta, two Spanish
dependencies in
North Africa, from
Málaga and Algeciras
respectively. There are
also ferry and hydro-
foil services from
Algeciras and
Benalmádena to
Tangier. Cruise lines
call at Málaga,
Algeciras and, occa-
sionally, Motril.
Trasmediterranea:
✉ c/Juan Diaz 4,
Málaga,
☎ 95 222 4391.

What to Pack
Dress on the Costa del
Sol is **informal** with
many visitors spend-
ing most of their time
in beachwear. Respect,
however, should be
shown when entering
cathedrals and
churches and when
exploring out of the
way villages, which
tend to be inhabited
by old people. Some
of the smarter hotels
in Marbella have a
dress code of jacket
and tie and younger
people usually dress
up in the evenings to
visit the many night-
clubs. Golf clubs also
require the usual
golfer's dress code.
Walking boots are
advisable for hiking in
Las Alpujarras and the
Serranía de Ronda,
and visitors should
remember that the
climate can be a lot
cooler at altitude.
Department stores
stock all major items.

Money Matters
Currency: Spain is a
member of the
European Union and

the currency is now the **Euro**.

Banks: Banking hours are ☺ 09:00–14:00 Monday–Friday and 09:00–13:00 on Saturdays, although they vary occasionally from branch to branch.

Credit Cards: All major credit cards are accepted although some country restaurants in villages and small tapas bars may require cash.

Holders of cards bearing the **Visa**, **Mastercard**, **Cirrus** and **Plus** signs can use Spanish automatic tellers, which have instructions in English.

Currency Exchange: Foreign currency and travellers' cheques can be changed in **banks** and at the **Bureaux de Change** which operate in the main resorts.

Taxes: Spanish sales tax (**IVA**) is currently 16% and is not always included in the price.

Tipping and Service Charges: Tipping is optional; around 10% of the price of a meal is acceptable. Petrol pump attendants and taxi drivers also expect a small tip.

Transport

Air: Domestic flights are operated by **Iberia**, its subsidiary **Viva Air** and **Aviaco**, with an efficient network linking Spain's major cities. Domestic flights operate from Málaga, Granada, Sevilla and Jerez.

Road: Southern Spain has an efficient dual-carriageway network, much improved since the Expo in Sevilla in 1992. Some *autopistas* in Spain are toll roads but the only section in Andalucía to carry a charge is between Sevilla and Jerez. Málaga and Sevilla both have ring roads and signposting everywhere is good, even on the mountain roads. Speed limits are 120kph (75mph) on *autopistas*, 120, 100 or 80kph (75, 62, 50mph) according to signs on *autovias* (dual carriageways), 90kph (56mph) on country roads and 60kph (37mph) on urban roads. Stiff, on-the-spot speeding fines are not uncommon. Wearing of seatbelts is compulsory in the front and, if fitted, in the back. Motorcyclists must wear safety helmets by law.

Rail: *see* page 87.

Bus: Private bus companies provide regular links between major towns and all the outlying villages. **Alsina Graells Sur**, ☎ 95 284 1365, links Málaga with Córdoba and Granada, and covers routes from Málaga to the eastern Costa del Sol – Vélez-Málaga, Nerja and Motril. In the western Costa del Sol, **Automóviles Portillo**, ☎ 95 287 2262, links Málaga with Fuengirola, Marbella, Estepona and Algeciras, stopping at the villages in between, and also serves Ronda and Coín. Timetables and fares are available from all the tourist offices and bus stations.

Business Hours

Shops and businesses generally open at 09:00 or 10:00, then close for a *siesta* at 13:30 or 14:00. They reopen with afternoon hours from around 16:00–20:00. Some businesses start much earlier, at around 08:00, and work straight through to 15:00 with no *siesta*. Business hours also change in the summer. Big department stores now stay open all day but most supermarkets close for lunch. Lunch tends to be served between 13:00 and 16:00, with dinner from 20:00 (sometimes dinner is served earlier for the benefit of tourists) to 23:00. Bars and clubs stay open late on the coast – sometimes until 04:00.

Time Difference

Spain is an hour ahead of GMT in winter. From the last Sunday in March to the last Sunday in October, it is two hours ahead.

Communications

The international dialling code for Spain is ☎ +34. Each province has its own dialling prefix – Málaga, for example, is ☎ 95, and Cádiz ☎ 956. When dialling from within the province, include the prefix. The international code for Gibraltar is ☎ +350. Dialling from Spain, the prefix is ☎ 9567. Cheap rates are between ◷ 22:00 and 08:00. Public phones take telephone cards. To call overseas, dial ☎ 00 and wait for the tone to change before dialling the country code and the number. Telephone cards and stamps can be bought from **Telefónica** offices or **tobacconists**. **Post offices** are open ◷ Monday–Saturday, 09:00–14:00.

Electricity

The power system is 220V or 225V AC. Older buildings occasionally have 110V or 125V AC and should be treated with extreme caution. Two-pin plugs are used. Americans will need a transformer, and British visitors an adaptor.

Weights and Measures

Spain uses the metric system.

Health Precautions

An excess of **sun** and *sangria* are the worst health problems encountered by most visitors to the Costa del Sol. Use a high-factor sun protection cream, wear a hat and take special care during the height of summer. Tap water is safe to drink in Spain, although mineral water is available everywhere. A good mosquito repellant is recommended. Spanish pharmacists are able to dispense medicines often only available on prescription elsewhere. Opening hours are ◷ 09:00–13:30 and

17:00–20:30 (with the occasional half-hour variation). Every area has a duty pharmacy offering a 24-hour service, the address of which is displayed on the doors of the other pharmacies.

Personal Safety

Petty crime is the only likely problem travellers might encounter, although the big cities have their no-go areas at night. Follow normal precautions: don't leave anything in a car; be careful with purses and wallets; don't wear ostentatious jewellery and use the hotel safety deposit boxes. Remember that some inland areas are very poor, so bag snatching is more of a temptation. Sexual harassment is not generally a big problem and as the streets are always so busy at night, women travellers should feel quite safe walking around resorts.

Emergencies

Emergency numbers vary from town to town, although the **Policía Nacional** has one number ☎ 091 nationwide. Dial ☎ 092 for the **Policía Municipal**, or in Málaga, ☎ 95 221 2415. Some other emergency numbers for Málaga are:
Fire brigade, ☎ 080.
Medical emergencies, ☎ 061.

Etiquette

Topless sunbathing is acceptable on beaches but more modesty is appropriate around lakes and in national parks. There are two nudist beaches (*playa nudista*) on the Costa del Sol, at Estepona and outside Fuengirola.

Language

Castilian Spanish is spoken everywhere; the Basque, Catalan and Galician languages of the north are not heard in the south. On the Costa del Sol, **English** is widely understood.

Useful Phrases
My name is...
● *Me llamo...*
Do you speak English? ● *¿Habla usted Ingles?*
OK ● *Vale* (pronounced 'balay')
Hello ● *¡Hola!*
Please ● *Por favor*
Thank you ● *Gracias*
You're welcome ● *De nada*
How much is...? ● *¿Cuánto cuesta...?*
Please speak more slowly ● *Puede hablar mas despacio*
Where is...? ● *¿Dónde está...?*
What time does it leave/arrive in...? ● *¿A qué hora sale/ llega a...?*
It's too expensive ● *Es demasiado caro*
Can one...? ● *¿Se puede...?*
Is there...? ● *¿Hay...?*
There has been an accident ● *Ha habido un accidente*
Please fill the fuel tank ● *Llénelo, por favor.*

INDEX OF SIGHTS

GENERAL INDEX

GENERAL INDEX